Cleveland's
CATALOG OF COOL

THE COUNTRYMAN PRESS
A DIVISION OF W. W. NORTON & COMPANY
INDEPENDENT PUBLISHERS SINCE 1923

land's

CATALOG OF
COOL

MICHAEL MURPHY

AN IRREVERENT
GUIDE TO THE LAND

For information about permission to reproduce
selections from this book, write to Permissions,
The Countryman Press, 500 Fifth Avenue, New York, NY 10110

For information about special discounts for bulk purchases, please
contact W. W. Norton Special Sales at specialsales@wwnorton.com
or 800-233-4830

Manufacturing by Versa Press
Book design by Endpaper Studio
Production manager: Lauren Abbate

The Countryman Press
www.countrymanpress.com

A division of W. W. Norton & Company, Inc.
500 Fifth Avenue, New York, NY 10110
www.wwnorton.com

978-1-68268-042-1 (pbk.)

10 9 8 7 6 5 4 3 2 1

Dedicated to Tina Musgrave, mother of a high school friend, Doug Musgrave. While trying to track down Doug for my return trip to Cleveland, I came across his mother's obituary. Until then, I had no idea Tina Musgrave had been a Cleveland tour guide. The piece claimed she was "noted for her detailed and fascinating tours of Millionaires' Row" and a "guide for Lakeview Cemetery, and a volunteer guide for the Cleveland Convention Center. She was also a contributing writer for the Encyclopedia of Cleveland History." I'd always known her as just Doug's mom and sister of Cleveland Browns and Detroit Lions linebacker Mike Lucci. With my new knowledge, she seems like the Cleveland version of my New Orleans persona and the appropriate person to whom to dedicate this book.

Contents

Introduction

"Why, oh why, oh why-oh. Why did I ever leave Ohio?"
— *Betty Comden and Adolph Green lyrics from* Wonderful Town

I LEFT CLEVELAND FOR GOOD ON JANUARY 23, 1978, TO MOVE TO New York City. For me, it was a red letter day. I had grown up in the temperate suburbs, moving from Shaker Heights to Pepper Pike. As a high schooler, I and many classmates were desperate to get away from all the white picket fenced yards, the ice cream shop over the Chagrin waterfall, and the gazebo in the town square where the band played on the Fourth of July. For a sixteen-year-old, it was absolutely stifling Americana. Film-maker Jim Jarmusch, from neighboring Cuyahoga Falls, said, "Growing up in Ohio was just planning to get out." Looking back as an adult, I can now see the charm. In fact, writing this book and learning about the Dyngus Days, visiting the Museum of Sacred Statues, and tasting a Slyman's corned beef sandwich for the first time, I have almost fallen in love with Cleveland all over again. But, I am *NOT* coming back to those winters.

Back in high school, the further you got away after graduation, the cooler you were. Ray Kutash went to Colorado and was cool. Jeff Terhune left the country and moved to Alberta, Canada. He was cooler.

High-school-aged kids now scare me a little bit. I remember all that new testosterone coursing through my veins resulting in a rage where I just wanted to break things. My "gang" of Mouse Gordon, Smokey Nagel, Genius George, Crazy Legs Carlson, Lil Rich Ward, and No No Novak used to top off the burning fire inside by blowing up mailboxes with cherry bombs and M-80s.

Our record was twenty-eight mailboxes in one night. There was one mailbox in front of Marc Silberman's house that was impervious to our firecrackers. Rather than cheap metal, it was built of thick wood and looked like a colonial house for hamsters. Not to be beaten, we eventually sawed that mailbox down and lit it on fire. And we were "the good kids." I was captain of the football team, Mouse was captain of the cross country team, Genius captain of the track team. My "gang" went on to respectable colleges like Lehigh and Wesleyan. Marc Silberman went on years later to be the Mayor. I hope there's a statute of limitations on blowing up or burning down mailboxes.

Cleveland is a city where the river was so polluted it caught on fire (repeatedly) as did Mayor Ralph Perk's hair. Some of its greatest sports moments include The Drive, The Fumble, The Decision, and they are all heartbreaking. For nicknames, rather than the Big Easy or the Crescent City, Cleveland has been called The Mistake on the Lake and, failed attempt at self promotion, The Plum.

There is an unwritten but universally recognized rule that nicknames are bestowed upon you by others. You cannot give yourself a nickname. Mouse, Crazy Legs, No No, and Smokey all understood this. Smokey got his nickname the night of a party when he snuck full cans of Coca Cola into a bonfire. When one exploded, we all laughed uproariously at Smokey's blackened face. It looked like something out of the Little Rascals or Three Stooges. And then we rushed him to the hospital.

Smokey tagged me with my high school nickname, Huncher. I used to have to lift weights practically every day in order to maintain a two-hundred-pound football-playing weight. Otherwise I'd drift down to 175. I miss those days. Now I gain two pounds just looking at a fully dressed po-boy. When I was exhausted during workouts, I'd grab the front of my sweat soaked T-shirt with both hands and sort of hunch over. I never liked the nickname Huncher, but it beat my previous and unimaginative nickname, Murf.

Writing about Cleveland, I will at times be as merciless as I was writing about Port of Call, a burger joint in New Orleans that smells like disinfectant, or the Bone Lady, a psychic who credits her abilities by pointing out she foresaw the winner of the Super Bowl held in New Orleans. As I wrote in *Fear That*, that must make ESPN a psychic vortex, because Tom Jackson and Mike Golic, both from Cleveland, as well as many others at the network made the same prediction.

From age two until after college, I was a Clevelander. I was born in Detroit, not that I'm bragging. This means I can make fun of Cleveland the same way you can make fun of your mom's cooking and your buck-toothed brother, but outsiders cannot. Olivia Nuzzi, a political writer for the *Daily Beast, Politico*, and *New York* magazine, made fun of Cleveland as a Jersey girl. The online world of tweets rained down on her, hurling insults like "sewer rat." I hope not to face the same reactions.

Comedian Mike Polk, Jr., has made a career poking fun at Cleveland, but as one who actually lives in Cleveland. If Mike was in Los Angeles or New York, you might have even heard of him. In Cleveland, he was a struggling local comedian until his two "Hastily-made Cleveland Tourism" videos posted on YouTube and went viral. Now he is a struggling comedian with two viral YouTube videos.

Of his videos, he writes, "The Cleveland Tourism Board gave me 14 million dollars about 8 months ago to make a promotional video to bring people to Cleveland. As usual, I waited till the last minute and I ended up having to shoot and edit it in about an hour yesterday afternoon. I probably should have invested more time." The two videos celebrate "both of our buildings and [that] the sun comes out almost three times a year." "The Hastily Made Cleveland Tourism Video: 2nd Attempt" closes with Mike's words, "It could be worse. At least we're not Detroit. *[pause]* We're not Detroit!"

His "success" did allow him to move from Lakewood to a tonier community in Cleveland. Yes, there are tonier communities in Cleveland. On one of the first nights in the new neighborhood, a brick was thrown through his windshield and his GPS was stolen. Mike rants that it's "frustrating how accurately I probably helped the thieves get away."

It is my hope that through the inspiration of this book, someday you actually visit Cleveland, or you'll make the most of it when the Hopkins Airport is shut down during a winter storm and you end up stuck in Cleveland. If you've done Disney World to death, and if you've been to the Statue of Liberty and the Hollywood Walk of Fame, isn't it time to turn away from tourist traps for some real adventures in . . . Cleveland? As said by author Kurt Vonnegut, "Bizarre travel plans are dancing lessons from God."

Ready to dance?

GHOULARDI

Before writing anything else about LeBron James, or the Rock & Roll Hall of Fame, or the burning Cuyahoga River, I feel compelled to write about the man I consider the most quintessential of all Clevelanders of all time. He will be a recurring thread throughout this book.

Turn Blue, Purple Knif, Amrap, Stay Sick, Don't Jaywalk—Live Longer, Cool It with the Boom-Booms, Oxnard, What? A Knocking on the Phone, This You Won't BeLIEVE, Holy Pierogies, This Movie's So Bad You Should Just Go to Bed, Hey Group, Ova Dey, Get Your Gotchies On, Well That Stinks, Group We're Going to Have Some Fun Tonight, The Whole World's a Leaky Umbrella, Scratch Glass, Pa-a-a-arma!

If any of those words just listed make any sense to you, you are part of the few, the proud, the "Group" who grew up Ova Dey in Cleveland. These are some of the catchphrases used by late-night horror movie host Ghoulardi. He was, he is, he will forever be among the most influential of Cleveland personalities who ever passed under the city's perpetually overcast skies.

His impact cannot be overstated. If you watch Jim Jarmusch's films, you are seeing a director clearly influenced by Ghoulardi. If you are part of the under-the-radar worshippers of Pere Ubu, you are listening to musicians clearly shaped by Ghoulardi. And unless you believe in the Jungian collective unconscious, when you watch *Mystery Science Theater* or *Pee Wee Herman's Playhouse*, you are witnessing either people directly copying Ghoulardi or people copying other people who have copied Ghoulardi.

Ernie Anderson, a.k.a. Ghoulardi, was a radio and TV personality who had a hard time memorizing lines and an even harder time dealing with authority. He was fired from almost every job he ever had prior to Ghoulardi. Radio station WSKI in Burlington, Vermont fired him for making fun of the sponsors on air. In Providence, Rhode Island, he was fired for riding his motorcycle through the halls of the station, leaving tire tracks on the walls. And in Cleveland, he was fired from WHK radio immediately after the Christmas party. He was telling a long elaborate joke and, just as he was about to deliver the punch line, his boss cut in and said it. Ernie looked at him and said indignantly, "Why did you do you that?" His boss' answer, "I anticipated it," prompted Anderson to respond, "Anticipate this: Go fuck yourself."

His next job was at Cleveland's WJW television. His gig as afternoon movie host on *Ernie's Place* featured live skits with his friend and comedy partner, Tim Conway. When Steve Allen "stole" Conway, who would go on to greater fame on *McHale's Navy* and the *Carol Burnett Show*, *Ernie's Place* was eventually shelved. The TV station still had to pay Anderson the balance of his contract, so they convinced him (twisted his arm) to become the Friday night horror host for an additional $65 per week.

While he wasn't initially enthusiastic about hosting movies he personally hated, Anderson came to realize having a show that was live TV, and in a late-night slot when basically no one in management was still awake, gave him the freedom he'd always needed. During this time, most American cities had their version of a local horror host: Zacherley in Philadelphia, Sir Graves Ghastly in Detroit, Morgus the Magnificent in New Orleans, Vampira in Los Angeles. Almost all typically portrayed themselves as mad scientists, vampires, or other horror film stock characters.

Ernie Anderson turned this established style of horror host on its severed head. Rather than affecting a phony Count Floyd type accent or draping himself in a vampire cape with cheesy make-up. Ghoulardi was a hipster who wore a clearly slapped-on fake Van Dyke beard, sunglasses missing one lens, wild hair, and a long white lab coat covered in promotional pins. He was insistent on the disguise because he didn't want to be recognized as something so low as a horror movie host, fearing that could damage his career.

But it wasn't his look that set him several continents apart from the rest, it was his attitude. Ghoulardi may have been the first host, or what's more, first TV spokesperson in any format, to insult the products he was pushing. The early to mid-'60s were much more apple-polished and sincere times. The biggest shock of his show named *Shock Theater* was what came out of his mouth.

In the spirit of "dance as though no one is watching," Ghoulardi did and said whatever came into his subversive mind late Friday nights. He'd introduce the week's movie by saying, "If you want to watch a good movie, don't watch this one," or, "This movie is so bad, you should just go to bed." His irreverence was refreshingly different from all the shill-meisters on other channels. Cleveland's other hosts at the time were Captain Penny, a man dressed in a railroad engineer outfit who performed utterly banal bits in between the Little Rascals and Three Stooges, and Barnaby, an elf with a straw hat, ascot, and blazer who lived in the Enchanted Forest with his invisible parrot, Long John. Barnaby had a thirty-year run on TV, give or take the numerous times Woodrow the Woodsman had to sub when Linn Sheldon, the real life Barnaby, went into detox. The only amusing part of Barnaby's show was watching how the TV station and grown-ups tried to double-speak around the host's sudden "vacations."

Ghoulardi's *Shock Theater* made him an instant star that quickly became a supernova. Spurred on by his unexpected success and by his late-night buddies on the set, Ghoulardi kept pushing the envelope. He developed his own hipster language, which was quoted at the beginning of this profile. Hating rock 'n' roll, Anderson filled the background with the coolest music ever heard on TV. He twisted up our young minds, introducing jazzy artists like Duane Eddy, Baskerville Hounds, Booker T. and the MG's, Jimmy McGriff, Les Cooper and the Soul Rockers, Lonnie Mack, Oscar Peterson, and novelty songs like the Trashmen's "Surfin Bird" ("Well a bird bird bird, bird is the word") and "Papa-Oom-Mow-Mow" by the Rivingtons.

I fell deeper in love with the show when, in addition to cool music, they started inserting soundtracks and drop-ins of Ghoulardi himself right into the movies. This was forty years before *Mystery Science Theater 3000*. Seeing Ghoulardi superimposed on the screen, running from the Giant Behemoth or telling Flash Gordon to follow him around the corner, was revolutionary. He included video clips of train crashes, toothless men gumming for all they were worth, pre–Wright brothers flying machines crashing to the ground, and audio clips of air horns blaring as rocket ships flew by or a comedian's voice exclaiming, "Dis man is DEAD!" when a body was discovered in the horror film. He got minor pushback when his hands cupped the enormous breast of the 50-Foot Woman.

Then his trashing of the movies morphed into Ghoulardi's trashing of anyone he didn't view as authentic or cool. His targets included bandleader Lawrence Welk, mayor of Cleveland Ralph Locher, and Cleveland's local television personalities such as singer/talk-show host Mike Douglas, plus Barnaby and Captain Penny. His most scurrilous remarks were reserved for the legendary (and prudish) local news commentator Dorothy Fuldheim. He called the seventy-year-old institution "Dorothy Baby." Their feud took on the dimension of a championship bout billed as between "the Beatnik and the Empress of News."

Ghoulardi started airing a series of taped skits called "Parma Place," which featured Anderson and his director, Chuck Schodowski, playing stereotypical ethnic Parma residents, i.e., Polish people. Ernie Anderson disliked 'white' suburbs like Parma almost as much as he loathed rock 'n' roll and station managers. The outfits in the skits always included ethnic-bashing white socks worn with black pants and dress shoes. Each Friday night, and several times each Friday night, Ghoulardi found a way to weave the word "Parma" into his two-hour show. He belted it as a stretched out: "PA-A-A-ARMA!" Then, each time he said Parma, Frankie Yankovic's polka song "Who Stole the Keeshka?" would strike up on the airwaves.

The mayor of Parma complained to station management. Parma residents found it particularly humiliating when Parma High School played basketball games and fans of the opposing team would toss white socks on the gym court. Under pressure, the station forced Anderson to discontinue the "Parma Place" skits.

And that was about the only interference the station ever inflicted on the hit show. In a reprise of an earlier subversive act, Ernie Anderson rode his motorcycle through the halls of WJW, ending up in the news director's office. He also added incendiary acts when he initiated new regular bits of blowing up model cars, statues, and other items sent in by viewers, with M-80s and cherry bombs. Their possession was illegal in Ohio. One time a bomb sent in by a viewer caused the set to burst into flames. His only reprimand from the network was a note that used one of his own catchphrases, "Cool it with the boom-booms."

He was far too popular to discipline. The station lived in mortal fear of what he might do on live TV, but his ratings were so high, they chose not to mess with the formula. To paraphrase another horror host, Ghoulardi could stand in the middle of Euclid Avenue and shoot somebody and he wouldn't lose any viewers . . . well, other than the one he just shot. Because everyone in Cleveland was watching Ghoulardi.

Ghoulardi scored 70 percent of the late-night audience. 70 Percent! His ratings were 27. The next nearest show in Cleveland was Johnny Carson's *Tonight Show*. It rated a 7. Fans sent up to one thousand pieces of mail a day. The police department attributed a 35 percent decline in crime on Friday nights in Cleveland to the fact that everyone was propped in front of a TV, watching Ghoulardi, rather than prowling the streets. Ghoulardi was King of Cleveland.

Storer Broadcasting, owners of WJW, sought to fully capitalize on (i.e., brand) Ghoulardi's huge audience with a comprehensive merchandising program. All over Cleveland Ghoulardi pins, bumper stickers, and book covers were the hottest thing a local kid could own. I mean in Cleveland they were way more cool than Air Jordans or Star Wars action figures would ever become. Manners, the local Big Boy franchise, cut a deal lucrative to both Ernie Anderson and their burger joints when they started selling their Turn Blue Ghoulardi shake, served in a blue plastic cup printed with Ghoulardi's face.

Looking back, probably the most amazing thing is how briefly the show was actually on the air. Ghoulardi's run lasted only from January 13, 1963, through December 16, 1966. It seems to have occupied my entire life from birth to college and steered me and many others into our ongoing desire to "Stay Sick" and forever be part of the "Group."

Ernie Anderson himself grew tired of being Ghoulardi. He didn't want to go through his forties still spewing "Turn Blue" and "Purple Knif." Encouraged by his buddy Tim Conway, Anderson left Cleveland for Los Angeles. He would go on to become the world's most famous and highest-paid announcer, earning as much as $2 million a year as the smooth, baritone voice of ABC-TV. Think of "*The Luuuuuuvv Boat.*" That was Ernie Anderson.

His impact from those four years as Ghoulardi, ending in 1966, continues to this day.

Film director Jim Jarmusch of *Stranger Than Paradise, Ghost Dog,* and *Broken Flowers,* credits Ghoulardi: "He was this great influence on me. There was this anarchism and wildness about him, this outsider hipster, this anti-authoritarian, blowing things up with explosives, that affected me as a little kid." He adds, "Then he'd insert himself in the movies and warn the viewer, 'Look out, kids, the crabs are coming.' It blew my mind." Jarmusch also points to Ghoulardi's soundtrack. "He opened me up to all kinds of weird-ass music," adds Jarmusch, whose *Stranger Than Paradise* uses (abuses) a Ghoulardi staple, Screamin' Jay Hawkings's "I Put a Spell on You."

Before the Sex Pistols formed in London, before CBGB opened in New York, Cleveland really was the heart of the new punk movement, with the Dead Boys, Easter Monkeys, Rocket From the Tombs, Pere Ubu, and the Electric Eels. Tin Huey, Pagans, and The Cramps all cite Ghoulardi as their spiritual guru. "We were all Ghoulardi Kids," asserts David Thomas, singer for Pere Ubu. "Someone asked me what my influences were," says guitarist and founder of the Electric Eels, John Morton. "Ghoulardi was a great influence. He was really an iconoclast in the true sense of the word, you know, in breaking established things. It was great for kids, this kind of defiance."

The Cramps named their 1990 album *Stay Sick!* and dedicated their 1997 album, *Big Beat From Badsville,* to Ghoulardi's memory.

The Akron-based band The Black Keys also paid homage to a Ghou-lardi catchphrase with their 2014 album *Turn Blue*.

Ernie Anderson's son, film director Paul Thomas Anderson, named his production company "The Ghoulardi Film Company." He has made clear the climactic fireworks scene in his film *Boogie Nights* was inspired by his dad's use of explosives.

John Petkovic, musician and writer for *The Plain Dealer*, summed it up best: "Ghoulardi altered the gene pool, leaving a legion of freaky followers to continue in his wake."

CHAPTER ONE

The Invention of Cleveland

HOW THE THE MISTAKE ON THE LAKE BECAME THE LAND

The rest of the country is perversely wont to misunderstand Cleveland.

—*Mark Winegardner*

O N JULY 22, 1796, SURVEYOR MOSES CLEAVELAND PADDLED UP to a landing where the Cuyahoga River met Lake Erie and he saw that it was good. The area would become known as Cleveland after a newspaper incorrectly spelled his name in 1831. Some say the misspelling was intentional because the paper needed to drop a letter to fit the space on their headline. This was nearly two hundred years before the Cuyahoga River famously caught on fire (repeatedly). Lake Erie has also been declared "dead," not because it was void of life but because the surface had too much life. Fed by industrial chemicals, bacterial life blossomed on the surface, suffocating most fish and aquatic life below under a blanket of slimy organisms.

After staying two days and founding the city, Cleaveland himself immediately went back to Connecticut, and he never came back.

There were only four settlers the first year: Nathaniel Doan, Lorenzo Carter, Job Phelps Stiles, and his wife, Tabitha Stiles.

The Great Lakes Scenic Tour is a scenic road system that connects Cleveland to Lake Erie

The population nearly doubled when David and Gilman Bryant came and opened a much-needed first distillery. They allegedly produced two quarts of raw spirits *every day*. That would seem to indicate those first few settlers remained pretty much buzzed, blitzed, blotto, and banjaxed at all times.

I first arrived in Cleveland in 1956. I was two years old. We'd come from Detroit after my father spent a few years in the Air Force; Michigan hospitals would require him to start his residency training all over, but a Cleveland hospital fast-tracked him to becoming a surgeon. Back then, Cleveland, Detroit, Buffalo, and Pittsburgh were basically all the same city: steel-based economies, populated by Eastern European immigrants, and you didn't see the sun for four months.

During my twenty-two years there, Cleveland was at one time a happenin' place. It was the sixth-largest city in America. It is now fifty-first. The Terminal Tower was the tallest skyscraper in America outside New York City. It is now seventy-fifth and not even the tallest building in Cleveland. The Key Tower (ranked twenty-fifth) is nearly two hundred feet taller. It was a medical hub, with the Cleveland Clinic at one time ranked as one of the best hospitals in the country, rated #1 in the treatment of cardio-vascular disease.

Before my time, it was even more of a happenin' place. In the late 1800s and early 1900s, Euclid Avenue was dubbed "Million-aires' Row." The elm-lined Street was mansion after mansion, built and owned by many of the wealthiest men in all of America. Neighbors included Isaac N. Pennock, the inventor of the first steel railway car; arc light inventor John Hay, personal secretary to Abraham Lincoln and Secretary of State under William McKinley; Jeptha Wade, founder of Western Union Telegraph; Worthy S. Streator, railroad baron, coal mine developer, and founder of the city of Streator, Illinois; and a wealth of other outrageously rich people, including the most famous of the bunch, John D. Rockefeller, the philanthropist who was probably the richest man in American history.

At one time, Rockefeller was interested in paying to establish a great university like Harvard or Yale in Cleveland. But civic leader J.L. Mather, who made his fortune in iron ore, convinced Rockefeller building a university would be wasted on the dull-witted working people of Cleveland. Rockefeller instead went on to fund his dream by establishing the University of Chicago.

Then the city really pissed him off by trying to double up his taxes. In so doing, Cleveland made a lifelong enemy. Rockefeller donated most of his wealth to New York City and issued a quote in 1914 that was perhaps more of a curse: "Cleveland ought to be ashamed to look herself in the face."

Charles F. Brush and John D. Rockefeller had ordered their houses be razed after their deaths because they preferred the destruction of their homes over the inevitable deterioration. The city seemed to follow their lead, as most of the once sprawling mansions along Euclid have been knocked down and replaced

Built in the 1920s, the Terminal Tower was the tallest building in the US
outside of New York City until 1964

by parking lots and storefronts where you can get a quick loan or trade in your cell phone for cash.

Back in 1884, Cleveland could lay claim to being the oil capital of the world. There were more oil refineries here (eighty-eight) than anywhere else. A few years later, Cleveland, not Detroit, became the Automobile Capital of the World. On March 24, 1898, the first commercial sale of an automobile happened in Cleveland. Scottish immigrant Alexander Winton had previously manufactured bicycles, but by the mid-1890s, he became interested in designing automobiles. At one point, the Winton Motor Car Co. employed some 1,500 people and had branches in London, Toronto, and Honolulu. Winton unfortunately saw the future of the car business as magnificently hand-produced vehicles, one at a time. He felt producing fewer cars would create a pent-up demand by the wealthy, enabling him to charge more for each vehicle.

When Henry Ford wanted to come and work with him, Winton thought Ford was a crackpot and didn't hire him. The Mistake on the Lake was so close to having the much cooler nickname of Mo-Town.

In the 1940s, Cleveland was set to be the center of aeronautics. Talented young engineers and pioneers in the fledgling aircraft industry came to Cleveland to design and build the country's first bomber. Among them were Donald Douglas, Larry Bell, and Dutch Kindleberger. They would go on to start McDonnell Douglas, Bell Helicopter, and Rockwell International. But none of this blossomed in Cleveland because local leaders, bankers, and politicians saw no future investing in aircraft once World War II was over.

A retired NASA official claims: "There was a window there, when Cleveland could have reached out and taken a major part of the space program." But they were outmaneuvered by a wily and willful Texas senator, Lyndon B. Johnson. As part of his pitch, LBJ said Houston was closer to the moon than Cleveland.

During my time in Cleveland, *Cosmopolitan* magazine ran a feature article in 1963 titled "The Good Life in Shaker Heights." The piece declared the Cleveland suburb to be the closest thing to a utopian society as could be found anywhere in the US.

All of Cleveland was surrounded by a wonderful series of parks, nicknamed the Emerald Necklace and designed by William Stinchcomb. He believed urbanites needed access to wilderness in order to maintain a healthy and balanced life. Cleveland's Metropolitan Parks became the model for urban planning in many other American cities.

At one time Cleveland was a happenin' place. And then, everything changed.

On a more serious side (I won't stay here long), Cleveland, like many cities, erupted in racial unrest and uprisings in the late '60s.

In a scenario that played out almost like a real-life version of Spike Lee's *Do the Right Thing*, Cleveland changed on the oppressively hot night of July 18, 1966. The Seventy-Niner's Cafe on the corner of East 79th and Hough Avenue was a bar owned by two white brothers, Dave and Abe Feigenbaum, set right in the heart of Cleveland's black community. The Feigenbaum brothers had already had some run-ins with area residents.

On this night, according to one account, a young prostitute came into the bar to solicit money from patrons to buy flowers for the funeral of a fellow working girl. She was abruptly thrown out and allegedly called the n-word. Another account stated that a black man came into the bar asking for water and was refused in a similar fashion. Whatever happened, the Feigenbaums claimed that they were not in the bar at the time. In any event, tensions had built to a pitch in recent weeks with protests of segregated school systems. White Murray Hill residents took to the streets to block efforts to integrate their local school. A minister was accidentally killed by a bulldozer as he sought to block the building of a new and segregated school. The newspapers buried these stories under more pro-Cleveland ones.

The kindling made of repressed anger and the onerous heat set the stage. The eviction of the black prostitute from the white-owned bar became the spark that erupted into the Hough Uprising. Hundreds of fires swept through the neighborhood. The night caused millions of dollars in damage. Gunfire left four dead, and dozens more were injured.

Rather than quelling the rage, the city papers made matters worse by insisting the uprising had to be caused by outsiders—black nationalists, maybe even communists.

Pre-riots, downtown Cleveland was the hub for shopping at the large department stores: the May Company, Higbee's, Halle's, and stores along Euclid Avenue. The signature event each Christmas season had been the lighting of the sixty-foot Sterling Lindner-Davis Christmas tree.

After the riots, white dollars stayed away from downtown, redirected to new suburban malls, such as Severence Center. Sterling Lindner-Davis closed in 1968. The other large department stores downtown would follow. The most painful for me had to be the decline of Halle's. The department store stood 195 feet high with a white terracotta facade. By Cleveland standards, it was the Taj Mahal. Every holiday season between Thanksgiving and Christmas, Halle's would roll out their promotional spokesperson, Mr. Jingeling. He was a balding elf with a huge ring of keys on his thick black belt. Any kid who grew up in Cleveland in the '50s and '60s can probably still today recite his theme song.

More than my personal disappointment in the loss of Mr. Jingeling, the white flight took many businesses and a great deal of consumer dollars away from the inner city. It would be like if Macy's and Bloomingdale's in Manhattan lost all their business to Long Island or the Paramus Mall.

At this same time, the city seemed to have a gift for making a fool of itself. Cleveland became a city version of the pratfall or spit take, an easy laugh as the butt of second-rate jokes told by third-rate comedians on *The Tonight Show* or *Merv Griffin*.

Cuyahoga River Flats

Richard Little gave the city a shot when performing at Ronald Reagan's inauguration ball. He advised Poland that if the Russians started to invade to change the name to Cleveland because no one ever goes there.

It wasn't as though Cleveland didn't do its part to lob up more than enough softballs of material for the jokes.

Mayor Ralph Perk, a high school dropout, caught his hair on fire when he attempted to use a welder's torch for a ribbon-cutting ceremony.

Mayor Perk's wife, Lucille, made the national news when she tried to get out of a gala with President Nixon and the First Lady by remarking to her husband, "Do you mind if I don't go? It's my bowling night."

Another Mayor named Ralph, Ralph Locher, became infamous by being the only person to stop a Beatles concert in the middle of the show, scolding the audience like an irate assistant principal and telling them, "The show won't continue until you all sit down."

Then there was Balloonfest. A United Way fundraiser decided to release 1.5 million helium balloons from Public Square to break the world record, set the previous year in Anaheim, California for Disneyland's thirtieth anniversary. The actual event turned into a balloon version of Altamont. The millions of balloons shut down the city's lakefront airport, were said to cause several drownings on Lake Erie when Coast Guard planes were unable to respond to distress calls, and littered beaches with thousands of deflated balloon carcasses as far as Ontario, Canada. Louise Nowakowski sued the city for $100,000, claiming her prize Arabian horses suffered permanent injuries when they were spooked by balloons.

Most famously, the Cuyahoga River caught on fire (repeatedly). A river bursting into flames is always good for a guaranteed laugh. For Clevelanders, it is also a lasting and annoying one. Ask anyone in the country to name three facts about Cleveland and the Cuyahoga River catching on fire, an event now more than fifty years in the past, will always make the list.

As grade school kids, we were forced to suffer field trips down the Cuyahoga. Teachers tried to teach us about draw section and swinging bridges, plus the viaducts and the spot where Moses Cleaveland set foot on shore where the city would be named after him, minus the "A." We kids, however, were mostly focused on the horrible smells as we rode past the sulfur mills, then asphalt, petroleum, salt, and steel. My second grade teacher told us Cuyahoga comes from the Mohawk word "Cayagaga," for "crooked river." My fourth grade teacher said the Senecas called it "Cuyohaga," or "place of the jawbone." Cayagaga or Cuyohaga, we just wanted to get back on the bus and go home.

The June 22, 1969, river fire captured the national attention of *Time* magazine's front cover story, which described the Cuyahoga as the river that "oozes rather than flows." Though for their dramatic cover image, having no photo of the fire, the magazine stretched journalistic integrity just a bit by rolling out an old photograph from the earlier and much worse fire in 1952.

Docks at the Cuyahoga River

While I lived in the city, the population topped 900,000 residents. It was consistently the sixth- or seventh-largest city in America each year. Today, it's 388,000 residents rank it fifty-first. Wichita, Kansas has one thousand more people than Cleveland.

The white flight of the '60s hurt the downtown area, but at least the flighty whities remained in the area. The '70s were far more devastating as once thriving steel and auto industries turned into the Rust Belt. Cleveland lost longstanding Fortune 500 businesses White Motors (dating to 1906), Reliance Electric (1905), Midland-Ross (1894), Warner & Swasey (1881), Standard Oil (1870), and Republic Steel (1866).

Cleveland became the first large city in America to declare bankruptcy, defaulting on its loans in 1978.

Civic pride wasn't much helped when *Forbes* magazine named it "the most miserable city in America."

Ever since the decades-long economic crash, Cleveland has been trying to reinvent itself. The city has had more nicknames than Shaquille O'Neal, a.k.a. Shaq, Shaq Fu, Shaq Daddy, The Diesel, Big Aristotle, Big Baryshnikov, Wilt Chamberneezy, and many many more.

The Cleveland Electric Illumination Co. coined the first in 1944. Their motto, "The Best Location in the Nation," was adopted by city leaders as Cleveland's slogan. In the 1970s, a Cleveland custom T-shirt company, Daffy Dan's, is largely credited with rebranding the city through the slogan, "Cleveland—You've Got to Be Tough!" While such a motto may bolster local civic "Bring It On" pride, it plays less well with tourists and conventioneers, as it seems to imply something like, "Come to Cleveland. But Bring Your Brass Knuckles."

A footnote: I learned during my return trip that Daffy Dan's did not actually coin "You've Got to Be Tough." They bought the rights from the estate of T-shirt maestro Chuck Ortega. Ortega was killed in an auto accident. When Cleveland went bankrupt, Ortega had created another shirt inscribed, "Defaults Not Mine."

In 1977, Ian Hunter wrote the song "Cleveland Rocks!" Columbia Records initially refused to release the song until he changed title and lyrics to "England Rocks!" They worried they'd sell less than a dozen copies of the song as initially conceived. Two years later, Hunter finally got to release his song as originally intended. "Cleveland Rocks!" became the city's anthem, played every Friday at 6:00 pm on local and iconic radio station WMMS. The song was later used as the theme song for the TV series set in Cleveland, *The Drew Carey Show*.

Cleveland's newspaper, *The Plain Dealer*, initiated a new slogan campaign in 1981. Choosing a winner, the paper sent all 468,000 Sunday subscribers bumper stickers that read, "New York's the Big Apple but Cleveland's a Plum." The motto began

The Rock and Roll Hall of Fame began inducting artists in 1986, but had no home until this building was constructed in 1993

popping up on buttons and T-shirts. Cleveland Mayor George Voinovich threw out the first plum at an Indians-Yankees game. The basic problem was that you don't hype your city by comparing it to an implied better city. Calling Cleveland "The Plum" was a veiled admission: *We're not New York*. It'd be like the old Houston Oilers of Earl Campbell and Dan Pastorini raising a banner at their stadium: "The Greatest Team to Never Make It to the Super Bowl—Damn Those Steelers!"

Positively Cleveland, the city's tourism agency, decided after some alleged research that the slogan "Cleveland Rocks!" did not appeal to travelers. Positively Cleveland seems to believe the word "Rocks!" caused the problem. I believe the bigger problem was that first word, "Cleveland."

Other nicknames have included "The 216," which was the city's area code. "The Cleve" was used by the TV show *30 Rock* and almost nowhere else. The longwinded "Metropolis of the Western Reserve" was a nineteenth-century nickname that gratefully went out of style. And there are the rarely used C-Town, City of Light, Sixth City (now Fifty-First City), CLE (the airport code), Forest City (back when it was blanketed in trees), America's North Coast (which could likewise apply to Beecher Falls, Vermont and International Falls, Minnesota), the much hated Mistake By the Lake, Believeland, or the now shortened and much preferred, The Land.

Positively Cleveland, which in 2014 rebranded their own company, changing their name to Destination Cleveland, has tried to create campaigns that highlight benefits and things to do in Cleveland rather than merely catchy slogans.

One campaign read, "This is Cleveland, where you don't need to move mountains to make a reservation or find parking." My first reaction was probably not their goal. I felt, "So, like . . . nobody's there?"

Cleveland can now boast the Rock & Roll Hall of Fame and a revitalized Playhouse Square (now the second largest performing arts center that's not in New York City), which hold's the unverified record for world's largest outdoor chandelier.

Almost as impressive is something so seemingly banal as a new grocery store. Heinen's, Cleveland's regional grocery chain, opened their new 33,000-square-foot flagship store in 2015 inside a former bank and landmark right downtown (900 Euclid Ave). The gorgeous building was designed in 1908 by George Browne Post, architect of the New York Stock Exchange. The most noteworthy feature is a grand rotunda, eighty-five feet high with stained glass, and bordered by thirteen murals depicting the history of the region by the painter Francis Davis Millet, who died on the Titanic.

Heinen's of Downtown, *a grocery store*, has received over 350 TripAdvisor ratings.

But what shocks me and impresses me is the old formerly burning river. The Cuyahoga River that used to make school kids gag on field trips now hosts the Dragonboat Festival, with nearly five hundred paddlers racing down a river that years ago would have disintegrated their skiffs by the third or fourth stroke. The Western Reserve Rowing Association uses the Cuyahoga River as their home base. The Burning River Fest has been around the last fifteen years as an annual two-day event that draws thousands to crowd along the river's edge for live music and beer.

The outside world seems to be noticing the new Cleveland. *The New York Post*, famous for their headlines like "Headless Body in Topless Bar," noted, "Cleveland is seeing a revival." *Fortune Magazine* called Cleveland a "new Brooklyn." They meant that as a cool-trendy compliment, though Cleveland State student Evan Schultz reacted, "I don't think they want to be another Brooklyn.... They just want to be Cleveland."

Between college and grad school, I briefly worked for a research company that was leased out to city agencies for special projects. My most enjoyable assignment was working for the Cleveland Transit Authority. Their task was to figure out where the hell all their bus stops were located. They'd lost track. I drove every street in Cuyahoga County and annotated maps with bus stop locations. I used different codes for a bus stop located on a corner versus mid-block and with a shelter or without. My work hopefully helped would-be passengers who'd been faithfully waiting at a stop where the busses previously never showed up.

The company now named Destination Cleveland has a mandate to push the image of the new and improved Cleveland to conventions and visitors. President and CEO David Gilbert revealed, "We've done a huge amount of research. We brought in the largest and best destination-branding firm in the world. They've done work from Barbados to Buenos Aires to Trump Hotels. It's a firm called MMGY Global, and they blew our whole committee away with their approach. They really did a lot of research of people's perceptions, and the fact is there's a visceral reaction to the word 'Cleveland.'"

Gilbert then boasted about their supposed fruits of their labor, "We can all look back and recall the pride we felt when we learned the city landed the coveted 2016 Republican National Convention, and those of us in the tourism industry won't soon forget earning the 2017 American Bus Association Conference."

I feel a certain amount of personal pride that before the American Bus Association came into Cleveland, I had helped the city avoid embarrassment by finding all of their bus stops.

CHAPTER TWO

Polish Boys & Popcorn Balls

THE CUISINE OF CLEVELAND

My father cried when I said I wanted to be a chef.

—Michael Symon, chef

S AN EX-CLEVELANDER, I WAS SURPRISED WHEN THE CAVA-liers unexpectedly ended a fifty-two-year drought of championships. As an ex-Clevelander, I was shocked seeing people happily paddling down the Cuyahoga River, which would have disintegrated their skiffs back in my day. But nothing prepared me to see Cleveland become a national culinary hub.

A recent issue of *Food & Wine* featured an eight page article dedicated to the restaurants of Cleveland. The piece was titled, "Meat Me in Cleveland." *Travel + Leisure* magazine ranked Cleveland as #7 among America's Best Food Cities.

During my years living in Cleveland, the height of haute cuisine was dining at Stouffer's on Shaker Square or at their top-of-the-town "skyscraper" restaurant. This was years before they became a frozen food empire and started peddling their three-and-a-half-minute meals.

In a 1960s Cleveland version of *très elegant*, Stouffer's served signature dishes like Lobster Newburg, and lobster mac and cheese, and cheese and ham crepes with no lobster, and their

Pierogies and cabbage noodles, a staple of Cleveland cuisine

noteworthy chicken pot pie, were known as "fat bombs," loaded with almost half their calories from fat and half a day's worth of sodium.

Stouffer's opened their first restaurant in 1924 at East 9th Street and Euclid Avenue. In 1968 they constructed a highly automated and modernized frozen food plant on a forty-two-acre site. The next year, Stouffer's new frozen food line got a huge marketing boost from NASA. Astronauts on Apollo missions signed up to dine on their food, leading to Stouffer's tag line, "Everybody who's been to the moon is eating Stouffer's."

On much rarer occasions, usually just when my grandmother was in town, she'd sneak us into the far more snazzy Kon Tiki restaurant inside the Sheraton Hotel. As kids with zero sense of decorum nor any moderation, we loved the over-the-top hanging lanterns, vibrant Asian print tapestries, bamboo curtains, and dried-up blowfish. Snarling six-foot-high statues of Polynesian gods guarded the entrance. We also loved that my grandmother would let us sneak sips from her fruity, super sweet, but highly alcoholic Zombie drinks. They were served in a plastic mug shaped like an island head hunter.

But our #1 hangout was Manners. Manners was the Cleveland version of the Big Boy chain, elsewhere called Elias Brothers, Frisch's, Shoney's, Elby's, Becker's, and Shap's. Big Boys were famous for the secret sauce on their double-decker cheeseburgers (basically Thousand Island dressing) and their strawberry pie, which was a slice of pie with one or two strawberries buried in a can and a half of strawberry glaze.

At their height, there were thirty-eight Manners in Cleveland. They crossed over from convenient diners to cool joints when they hooked up with horror movie host and local sensation Ghoulardi. Ernie Anderson, a.k.a. Ghoulardi, was a bit of a health nut and would never eat the food they served, but his did sign a contract for Manners to use his likeness. They created the Big Ghoulardi Shake. It was nothing more than their Orange Freeze with blue food coloring to reflect one of Ghoulardi's signature sayings, "Turn Blue!" Manners customers could get a bumper sticker or pin printed, "This Knif Drank a Manners Big Ghoulardi Shake." Knif is another Ghoulardi phrase. Knif is fink spelled backwards. After drinking the Big Ghoulardi, you got to keep the plastic blue glass, printed on the outside with his likeness and featuring a clear see-through cup bottom.

There were plenty of additional iconic spots we didn't go. The classy restaurants inside the large department stores seemed exclusively set aside for ladies' lunches. As a kid, I peeked inside the Silver Grille on a top floor at Higbee's and the Geranium Room inside Halle's, but I never once ate in them.

The old Woolworth's lunch counters were more my speed. There were plenty of other noted restaurants that simply weren't a part of my life because they were on "the wrong side of town."

There was this weird unwritten rule that East-Siders (like me) never crossed the Cuyahoga River to go to the West Side, and vice versa. Writer Scott Raab recollects, "East and West Siders didn't mix, save at ball games and Cleveland State University, where I met Wife One. Her parents had never set foot on the East Side until the day of our wedding." It's a bit like how New York City hipsters never cross above 14th Street, and starched-collared executives in Midtown never venture south. After the riots of '66, many of the Cleveland East Side restaurants in downtown were off-limits too.

I never once set foot in Miller's, an institution in Lakewood, known for their hot sticky buns just out of the oven and their chicken à la king. I now feel my childhood was deprived by not once going to Clark's for their meat loaf or pot roast, plus their treasure chest of toys set up for kids who cleaned their plates. I imagine the toys were no better than you'd get in a box of Cracker Jack or than what you'd scoop up with an arcade claw crane, but I'm disappointed that I'll never know for sure.

More than restaurants, my childhood food memories are about specific foods or brands. For many Clevelanders, Bertman Ballpark Mustard invokes passionately held memories as much as Junior's cheesecake for New Yorkers or Zapp's potato chips in my current hometown.

Their spicy, vinegar-based, brown mustard was the highlight

of every Indians game, certainly much more than anything you'd see on the baseball diamond. The distinctive mustard was created by Joseph Bertman in 1921. Bertman sold food products to schools, hospitals, and other large-scale operations like stadiums. His mustard became a hit at League Park, then the home of the Cleveland Indians. Bertman's was the mustard served at Cleveland Municipal Stadium for over sixty years. It is again served today at Cleveland's Progressive Field.

Locally, you can buy single jars of the mustard at Heinen's, Dave's Market, and other local grocery stores, plus area delis Corky & Lenny's, Davis Bakery & Deli, and Jack's Deli.

If you're not in Cleveland, you can still go to their website (bertmanballparkmustard.com) and order in bulk. However, you cannot order a single bottle to ship. Your options are a case of twelve 16-ounce bottles (for $44) or four 1-gallon containers (for $48).

When I first discovered the Bertman's website, I was a good fifteen years removed from Cleveland. I was so excited, I didn't hesitate to order the twelve bottles. Like a number of childhood memories, the reality didn't quite live up to my recollections. When I moved, three years later, I still had ten unopened bottles at the back of the cupboard. And they didn't make the move.

The popcorn ball is my vote for the most signature of signature foods from Cleveland. New Orleans invented Oysters Rockefeller, Oysters Bienville, Bananas Foster, the muffaletta, po'boys, pralines, and about a hundred other dishes. Philadelphia has their cheesesteaks, Boston their clam chowder, and Louisville, Kentucky the hot brown. Cleveland has the popcorn ball.

Long before Paula Deen adapted her popcorn ball recipe with two cups of sugar and a shortened-lifetime supply of butter, the original popcorn ball was invented by Dudley S. Humphrey II in 1897, who famously first sold them at Euclid Beach Amusement Park.

There is a myth (i.e., bald-faced lie) that the popcorn ball was invented in Nebraska. The legend claims popcorn balls were miraculously created when the scorching sunshine popped the kernels in the cornfields while the follow-up rain washed the syrup out of the sugarcane. The syrup flowed down the hill and rolled popped corn into great balls, some of them hundreds of feet high. Then, grasshoppers ate all the hundred foot high popcorn balls in one single day on July 21, 1874.

Euclid Beach Park was initially a bit shady, catering to a motley crowd hungering for "beer, freaks, fakes, chance games, questionable shows, and palmists." In 1901, Humphrey bought the park, intent on cleaning up its image and peddling their family-style popcorn balls.

Today, the Humphreys grow and process their popcorn on a five-hundred-acre farm in Wakeman, Ohio. They make about eight thousand popcorn balls a day using age-old techniques. Once dried, the kernels must sit for an additional two to three months to provide the best pop. Then they are mixed in syrup and cooled in copper kettles.

Like Bertman Stadium Mustard, Humphrey Popcorn Balls are easily bought at area stores in Cleveland, but for others you'll need to go on their website (www.humphreycompany.com) and order in bulk. The assortments of three-inch popcorn balls range in quantity from fifteen ($24.95) to one hundred ($51.95).

Slightly less signature is a Cleveland "delicacy" known as Polish Boys. It's a grilled, often deep-fried kielbasa on a toasted bun, topped with fries and slaw before being drenched in barbecue sauce. Virgil Whitmore, who opened the original Whitmore's Bar-B-Q back in the 1940s, is credited with creating the first Polish Boy. Whitmore combined all the ingredients he had on hand and came up with this delicious mess. It's The Land's version of New Orleans po'boy, or Philadelphia's cheesesteak, or Pittsburgh's Primanti sandwich.

These days, you can scarf Polish Boys in barbecue joints like Whitmore's (17121 Euclid Ave.), Freddie's Southern Style Rib House (15908 St. Clair Ave.), Hot Sauce Williams (3770 Lee Rd.),

Mabel's BBQ on E. 4th Street

Rib Cage (2214 Lee Rd.), and, widely touted as the city's favorite, Seti's Polish Boys food truck. Polish Boys can also be had, (called "Polish Girls," though) at Michael Symon's Mabel's BBQ (2050 E. 4th St.).

Esquire named Freddie's Polish Boy as one of the best sandwiches in America. *Food & Wine*, plus *Every Day with Rachael Ray*, picked Seti's as "the best," and Zagat, when choosing the best sandwich in each state, named Seti's Polish Boy as Ohio's. Seti's truck is parked in front of the Thomas F. McCafferty Health Center on Lorain Avenue near W. 42nd Street. They'll be parked there Monday through Friday from 10 a.m. to 3 p.m.

From a foundation of popcorn balls, stadium mustard, and Polish Boys, in the last few years, as I was living and focused elsewhere, Cleveland has undergone a revolution.

There are today nearly as many food festivals in Cleveland as there are in New Orleans. In Cleveland the food festivals focus on nationality more than a specific food. The Little Italy Feast of the Assumption in mid-August is a religious holiday celebrating, among other things, pasta and Peroni. The Romanian Festival is a three-day celebration with folk dancing, church tours, and plenty of mamaliga (a cheesy cornbread delicacy). Labor Day is accompanied by the Middle Eastern Festival with food and a competition for Best Hummus. The Serbian Cultural Festival has been going strong for eighty years. It's more feast than festival, with cheese strudel (gibanica), grilled meat (cevapi), and that potent plum brandy known as slivovica. The Russian Festival serves blini (Russian crepes), stuffed cabbage and pelmeni (Russian ravioli), and, of course, borscht.

There are also a few "normal" food festivals focused on food. The Pizza Festival is held in late June. It is a three-day fest at the Cuyahoga County Fairgrounds and draws over fifteen thousand attendees each year. The National Hamburger Festival is technically in Akron, thirty-nine miles to the South, honoring Akron as an old-fashioned burger joint kind of town. Places like Skyway, Swensons, Bob's Hamburg, and Hamburger Station line their streets. The burger blowout includes a hamburger-eating contest and a burger-bobbing contest. Bobbing contestants with arms held behind their back try to bob for burgers from vats of ketchup using only their mouths. I have never witnessed a burger-bobbing, but I envision something like the storming of Normandy Beach scene in *Saving Private Ryan*.

Michael Symon is the George Washington of the Cleveland food revolution. He's the shaved-headed chef on your TV with the on-again, off-again soul patch and the perpetually on-again goofy laugh. Named a Best New Chef by *Food & Wine* magazine, he has won *Iron Chef America*, become a regular on TV cooking shows, and opened a string of Cleveland restaurants as chef/owner, including Lola Bistro (chosen as one of "America's Best

Restaurants" by *Gourmet* magazine), B Spot Burgers (picked by *Bon Appétit* as one of the country's Top Tenburger joints), and Mabel's BBQ.

Wherever he goes and opens new restaurants, like Austin or Pittsburgh, his cuisine is always fully Cleveland. In this case, that's a compliment. There is a phrase, "Full Cleveland," which means a man displaying questionable fashion sense, pairing his white leather shoes with a white belt.

As the subject of the piece written in *Food & Wine*, Symon waxes poetic about the rich Old World history and charm of the many European markets selling headcheese at the Sausage Shoppe and the pierogies at Sokolowski's University Inn.

Chef Michael's website can inform you of his favorite kitchen instrument (the rasp), favorite TV show (*Ray Donovan*), and favorite guilty pleasure (salt and vinegar chips and Lawson's dip).

Lawson's was a local chain of convenience stores. Before 7-Eleven and Circle K dominated the eggs, milk, and Slim Jim market, every city had their own mini-chains like Dash In, Kangaroo Express, and Loaf 'N Jug. Anyone who grew up in Cleveland, and I mean *anyone*, can recite the Lawson's TV and radio jingle, "Roll on Big O. Get that juice up to Lawson's in forty hours."

Lawson's first opened in 1939 in Cuyahoga Falls. They were eventually bought out by a series of mega-Death-Star owners. The current owner is Daiei, a Japanese corporation with Mitsubishi as the main shareholder. They are now headquartered in Ōsaki. There are now 11,384 Lawson's stores in Japan, with others in Indonesia and China.

The good news for Michael Symon and other Clevelanders is that when when most of Lawson's locations were bought out and converted to Circle K's, a Cleveland-driven uprising forced the new owners to commit to continue selling Lawson's Chip Dip no matter the name of the store.

Cleveland has home-grown or lured in many other big-name chefs. Strongsville native Jonathon Sawyer embraces his Cleve-

The Greenhouse Tavern, very much a symbol of Cleveland's growth as a culinary city

land roots with pride. He cut his culinary teeth as a line cook in Miami and remembers it as "hearing people dog your hometown, you never forget that." As a full-grown chef, he returned to Cleveland. "Promoting Cleveland is very important to me," Sawyer notes. "When we announced the Greenhouse Tavern, it was very important for us that it was in downtown Cleveland." *Bon Appétit* picked Greenhouse as one of the "Best New Restaurants" in 2009.

After Greenhouse, he then opened Noodlecat, a hardcore Japanese restaurant that might have fit unnoticed in New York or San

Francisco, but was outright weird to Clevelanders at the time. "Five years ago, ramen noodles were foreign to Cleveland," Sawyer recalls. His third Cleveland restaurant is Trentina, featuring the cuisine of Trentino in Northern Italy, where Chef's wife, Amelia, is from. He also has quick food venues in both the Browns's stadium (Street Frites and Sausage & Peppers) and the Cavs's arena (See Saw Pretzel Shoppe).

Chef Sawyer has started stacking up awards, like *Food & Wine* magazine naming him "Best New Chef" in 2010, and in 2015 he took home the coveted James Beard award for Best Chef, Great Lakes.

In other ways, Jonathon Sawyer seems incongruous, at least with my memories of Cleveland. Like someone from Napa Valley, he grows herbs on his downtown restaurant's rooftop, and where I knew basements as the place for pool tables and unused exercise equipment, three hundred gallons of single-origin and barrel-aged wine, beer, and malt vinegars are fermenting in his. He recycles everything. He himself bikes to and from work each day.

Cleveland chef Rocco Whalen opened Fahrenheit in the revitalized Tremont neighborhood in 2002. At one time—like, 1900 time—Tremont was a Polish settlement with thirty-two Polish grocery stores and sixty-seven Polish saloons. Then the construction of Interstates 71 and 490 cut right through the neighborhood, sending many residents to more suburban communities. In the 1980s, artsy types, drawn by the Old-World feel of the neighborhood, helped transform Tremont into a desirable spot once again.

Fahrenheit was listed in *Gourmet* magazine among its "Guide to America's Best Restaurants." *Esquire* magazine touted Fahrenheit as one of the best new restaurants in America and Chef Rocco as a chef to keep an eye on.

If you can look away from Rocco long enough, you might see Matt Fish, another chef much-honored for his lifelong passion, grilled cheese sandwiches. He opened his signature restaurant, Melt Bar & Grilled, in 2006. They now serve more than five hundred grilled cheese sandwiches every day and as many craft beers. His are not ordinary grilled cheese sandwiches. Melt's variations include the Parmageddon, filled with cheddar, sautéed onion, vodka kraut, and potato pierogis, and The Dude Abides, which comes stuffed with provolone and romano, homemade meatballs, fried mozzarella, basil marinara, and roasted garlic.

Fish now has eight locations and has expanded to Columbus, Ohio. He's won honors from *USA Today* and *Esquire* magazine, and has been visited by Guy Fieri for *Diners, Drive-Ins and Dives* and Adam Richman's *Man v. Food.*

Dante Boccuzzi started working in Cleveland-area restaurants at age fourteen, I am guessing breaking several child labor laws. His training took him to London; Mougins, France; and Brescia, Italy. He returned to America to head the kitchen at San Francisco's Silks Restaurant, where he was twice nominated for the James Beard Rising Star Chef, then ran off to Italy again as the executive chef at Nobu Milan, then New York City, where he earned a Michelin star for Aureole Restaurant. Finally, his intense globe gallivanting led him back to his native Cleveland in 2007. Dante was his first restaurant, followed by Ginko in Cleveland, DC Pasta Co. in Strongsville, DBA (as in Dante Boccuzzi Akron), and more recently, Dante Next Door, in the space immediately adjacent to Dante, where he serves more casual fare.

Chris Hodgson's gallivanting was confined to Cleveland and the back of a truck. His food truck, Dim and Den Sum, was one of the first to hit Cleveland's streets. He developed an almost cult-like following. People scanned for the big red octopus with fangs spray-painted on the side of his truck. Fancy fish tacos were his thing. His second truck, the Hodge Podge, became the more nationally known as he trekked 3,500 miles on the Food Network show *The Great Food Truck Race.* Chris came in second place. Back off the road, he opened his first brick and mortar restaurant, Hodge's. There, he serves international comfort food like Korean fried duck wings, Thai chicken skewers, and blue crab hush puppies. He also makes Browns games slightly more bearable with a concession stand at their FirstEnergy Stadium called Hodgson's Downtown Dogs.

Douglas Katz has been called "the Alice Waters of Cleveland" for his commitment to fresh ingredients bought from local farmers' markets. His first restaurant, the Katz Club Diner, was originally an Art Deco style historic O'Mahony Diner, circa 1949. It was engulfed in flames October 2014, causing just under a million dollars in damage. He reopened the diner with his ongoing passion for what he termed "classic casual experiences from around the world." Featured dishes include Asian noodles, tacos, burgers and fries, Indian street food, and Southern fried chicken.

In 2014, the James Beard Foundation nominated Katz for best Chef of the Great Lakes Region.

Zack Bruell is the grizzled veteran of the current Cleveland food scene. He's been around for more than thirty years. *Cleveland Magazine* credits him with introducing the area to an emerging trend of bistro dining and fusion cuisine. He has opened six successful establishments, plus a restaurant-style catering and events company, Zack Bruell Events.

Parallax, located in the Tremont neighborhood, is Bruell's flagship restaurant, with a strong emphasis on seafood and sushi. Table 45 at the InterContinental hotel focuses on popular international street food. L'Albatros is a traditional French brasserie, Chinato is Italian, and Cowell & Hubbard is also a French restaurant located in the center of Playhouse Square. The non-French sounding name comes from the iconic jewelry store that used to occupy the space from 1920 to 1981. Dynomite is his far more casual burger joint, here named after the catchphrase of Jimmie "J.J." Walker on the '70s sitcom *Good Times*.

Except for Bruell's thirty-year run, Katz, Sawyer, Fish, Rocco Whalen, Dante Boccuzzi, Michael Symon, and the other chefs just listed forged the Cleveland culinary scene within the last fifteen to twenty years. This truly is nothing short of a revolution. Years ago, there was really only one notable chef in the entire city. You know him even if you're not a foodie. In fact, it's probably better if you're not a foodie.

Foodie is a terrible word anyway. There are arguments as to whether we should blame Gael Greene for inventing the word in her *New York* magazine column or if that infamy belongs to Ann Barr of the London magazine *Harper's & Queens*. I say a pox on both their houses for being first, second, or fifteenth to use it.

Ettore Boiardi immigrated from Piacenza, Italy in 1897. After passing through Ellis Island, Ettore and his brother Paolo got their first jobs in America working in the kitchen of the Plaza Hotel in New York City. Ettore worked his way up to head chef. He then moved to Cleveland to open his own restaurant, Il Giardino d'Italia, on East 9th Street and Woodward Avenue.

The patrons of Il Giardino d'Italia frequently asked Ettore for the recipe for his spaghetti sauce, which he would never give. But he did start selling samples of the sauce in washed-out glass milk bottles. This led to him to create a factory where his food could be mass-produced and sold to groceries across the country. To help Americans pronounce his last name, he sold his packaged food with a phonetically spelled out Chef Boy-ar-dee.

More than popcorn balls, Bertman's mustard, or any kind of cured meat, for some of us the most revered food of Cleveland is Hough Bakery's white on white cake.

At one time, years before the outburst of artisan and award-winning bakeries like François Payard Bakery in New York City and Tartine Bakery in San Francisco, each city had their local neighborhood bakers, places where you'd pick up a loaf of bread or cupcakes on the way home. These bakeries were never meant to get noticed by *Bon Appétit, Saveur,* or *Travel & Leisure.* They were most often thought of as stores of necessity, no more epicurean than stopping by a newsstand to pick up the day's paper or getting some replacement shoestring at the drugstore.

That didn't mean they weren't beloved. And Hough Bakeries,

Archie's Lakeshore Bakery, a spiritual successor to the much loved Hough Home Bakery

with their white boxes sealed with blue and white string, were nothing if not beloved. Their white on white cake was the staple for many Cleveland birthday parties, retirement parties, and quite a few weddings.

Lionel "Archie" Pile founded Hough Home Bakery in May of 1903, opening their first location at 8708 Hough Avenue. They opened with four employees, Archie's sons, Arthur, Lawrence, Kenneth, and Robert. Seventy years later, during my white cake eating days, Hough Bakeries had grown to over one thousand employees, with annual sales of $25 million.

However, the company fell on hard times due to a lethal combination of automation and the one-stop convenience of bakery counters popping up at grocers like A&P and Kroger's. There was also a disheartening consumer shift toward mass-produced goods from Hostess, Little Debbie, and their processed sugary hoard. This all replaced the need for a local bakery. Hough Bakeries closed the doors of all thirty-two locations for good on

August 8, 1992. It seemed as though Hough Bakery would join Mr. Jingeling, Ghoulardi, and Browns' championships as just fond memories of better times. There developed a "Fans of Hough Bakery" webpage where Clevelanders recalled eating their delicacies and shared the best attempts at concocted recipes.

Then, another Archie, Archie Garner, stepped up like an Aaron Rodgers or Dikembe Mutombo TV commercial: "Not in My House!" Archie had worked for Hough Bakeries for twenty-five years as a pastry chef and baker. He wasn't about to let the bakery go quietly. It was a part of his blood.

After Hough Bakeries went out of business, he began planning for his own bakery. "I went around to auctions buying used baking equipment, which I stored in my basement. To pay the bills, I worked part-time in various catering departments as well as doing odd jobs like planting flowers and washing walls."

Finally, he found a vacant former bakery in a sketchy part of Collinwood. The building still had a working oven. As soon as Archie signed the lease, he became concerned that no one would show up. He's now been there over twenty years. Almost from the beginning, business was brisk at Archie's Lakeshore Bakery (14906 Lakeshore Blvd.) with people flooding in from around the city, grateful to sample once again the baked goods from their memory. To help stoke those memories, Archie opened his shop with a gallery of historic Hough Bakery photos, authentic counters, and display cases once used at the bakeries, and (of course) Hough's "secret" recipes. He works the bakery alongside his wife, Valinda, and their two daughters, Sandy and Samantha.

One time, while Archie was working in the back of his bakery, he heard a customer crying out front. When he came up front, he discovered an elderly woman in tears. He asked what was wrong, and she replied the white cake was a part of her childhood that until today she thought she'd never get to taste again.

CHAPTER THREE

Ucztowanie!

WHERE TO CHOW DOWN IN CLEVELAND

There is no love sincerer than the love of food.

—George Bernard Shaw

*U*CZTOWANIE IS POLISH FOR FEASTING. IN MY BOOK, *EAT DAT*, I profiled just over two hundred restaurants in New Orleans. But that was an entire book. In this mere chapter, I'll get to about forty eating spots in Cleveland, with apologies to the hundreds more left out. The restaurants that are listed are shown by neighborhood. Needless to say, I couldn't (and didn't) actually eat at every one of these restaurants. If I don't mention the food, it's probably because I didn't eat there.

If you crave a far more expansive view of Cleveland's restaurants, I can enthusiastically suggest you pour over columns written by the city's premier food writer, Douglas Trattner. He is currently the dining editor of *Cleveland Scene*. His writings, which include food, beverage, travel, and culture, have been published locally, nationally, and internationally, and have appeared in *Food Network Magazine, Tasting Table, Eater, Thrillist, Miami Herald, Globe and Mail, Wine & Spirits,* and *The Plain Dealer.* Thanks to his writing relationship with Cleveland's premier chef, Michael Symon, he also now joins Stephen King and J.K. Rowling as a *New York Times* best-selling author.

When first mapping out my book, I wanted to interview Trattner but in an ironic way, as I thought a food writer and restaurant reviewer in Cleveland was as much needed as a party planner for the Amish. I, of course, know better now and apologize for my absentee nescience.

He did suffer some fools initially. He told me, "The typical response I'd get from folks living in the burbs or in other, larger, markets, was: 'Restaurant critic? In Cleveland!? What is there to write about?' The truth is it was a struggle at first. I'd mix new restaurant reviews with "classics" that deserved a fresh look. But before long neighborhoods like Tremont and Ohio City began to pop, plus there were always new places popping up all over town. Little did I know just how much would happen over the next fifteen years."

Trattner characterizes Cleveland cuisine: "The Midwest has been doing farm-to-table cooking ever since Jewish grandmothers made chicken livers with schmaltz and Hungarian moms stuffed ground pork into pig intestines. The best chefs in Cleveland take that premise and run with it, utilizing humanely raised animals and farmers-market produce to create approachable but compelling food. This sensibility has also given rise to modern craft butcher shops that harken back to the good old days."

DOWNTOWN

Blue Point Grille
700 W St. Clair Ave., 216-875-7827
Blue Point is consistently chosen as Cleveland's Best Seafood restaurant according to *Cleveland Magazine* and others. They shuck over seventy-five thousand fresh oysters per year. I hope

not to lose every reader I didn't already lose when I wrote the day I left Cleveland was a red letter day. I now live in a city that serves fifty thousand oysters *a day*. But Blue Point's happy hour serves $1 oysters and $1.50 crab claws, plus drinks by noted bartender Halle Bruno. Now that is impressive.

The Greenhouse Tavern
2038 E. 4th St., 216-443-0511

This is James Beard Award–winning chef Jonathon Sawyer's flagship. The website bills it as "A Rustbelt Revolution." He and his wife, Amelia, left New York in 2009 to come open a restaurant in Cleveland, Jonathon's hometown. Most friends and food colleagues probably thought he was nuts. Reading chef Jonathon's current menu online, with foie gras, steamed clams, and Nonna's meatloaf (Deejay's pork, cranberry, pistachio, fig, pickled mustard seed, and shaved lomo), my wife wanted to skip work and come with me on my return trip to The Land. Their most pricey entrée, the $56 roasted pig head in BBQ sauce with raw vegetable salad, seems more exquisitely Deep South than my pot roast years in Cleveland.

I went for lunch lusting for foie gras. I learned it's only served at dinner. My magenta-haired waitress suggested I order their award-winning wings. They replaced New Orleans's Primitivo duck wings as the best I have ever had.

Dynomite
1302 Euclid Ave., 216-298-4077

This original Dynomite operates seasonally at the US Bank Plaza in the entrance of Playhouse Square. They offer seven kinds of burgers, all priced $8. The namesake Dynomite Burger is jalapeno, red onion, pepper jack, and spicy mayo. The Cowell & Hubbard Burger, named after the iconic jewelry store, has Fontina, caramelized onions, smoked paprika mayo, and sherry vinegar. Or, you might choose the burger named after owner/chef Zack

Dante's rather dignified exterior is part of a former bank building

Bruell. The Big Zack is onions, peppers, white cheddar, chili fries, BBQ mayo, and cilantro. Another option is to choose the other locations. There's a Dynomite inside Progressive Field and Dynomite Burgers & Sushi (11500 Euclid Ave.).

Lola Bistro
2058 E. 4th St., 216-621-5652
If there is one restaurant that heralded in a new age of Cleveland restaurants, it's Lola Bistro. Michael Symon and his wife, Liz Shanahan, opened Lola in Cleveland's Tremont neighborhood in 1997 and moved it to the current and much larger location in 2006, where they now have an open kitchen, chef's table, private and semi-private rooms, and a glass-enclosed wine wall next to a sixteen-seat bar.

Symon and his restaurant have won about every award you can win. He was *Food & Wine* magazine's Best New Chef in 1997 and won the James Beard Award as Best Chef, Great Lakes Region in 2009. The restaurant received the Four Diamonds Award from AAA, *Metro Mix Cleveland*'s choice as Best Restaurant in Cleveland, *Cleveland Magazine*'s trifecta plus one of the Silver Spoon Awards for Best Fine Dining, Best Local Chef, Best Desserts, and Best Decor. Zagat shows Lola as the most popular restaurant in Cleveland.

Everyone loves Lola. Well, everyone except one reviewer on *Chowhound*. We learn online she's from Washington, DC. Other than that, we know she's a bit crabby. She posted and then continued to post whiny comments about her vegetarian risotto with butternut squash and tofu. She was eating at Lola for God's sake! The restaurant has a curing room for handmade sausages. Among the noted dishes are beef cheek pierogis. Symon himself describes his cooking as "meat-centric." Did she somehow miss the signs that risotto and tofu were not his sweet spot?

Her comments would be like me going to Momofuku and complaining they didn't serve chili cheese fries.

Authentic Cleveland BBQ items on offer at Mabel's

Mabel's BBQ

2050 E. 4th St., 216-417-8823

Right next door to Lola is another Michael Symon restaurant, Mabel's. It is decidedly and purposely Symon's most casual and affordable restaurant. Here, you can get your choice of what the menu describes as "Pig Parts"—crispy pig's ears, crispy tales, or cracklins—all for only $7. The most expensive item is a precipice of kielbasa and spare ribs piled with sauerkraut, enough to serve the entire Cavaliers team as a pre-game meal. It is called "This Is Cleveland" and costs a mere $19.

Mabel's serves most everything with self-described Cleveland-style barbecue. Their BBQ sauce includes Bertman Ballpark Mustard. They also serve Cleveland pickles and Cleveland kraut. I thought that was just a sales pitch thing, but then learned there is actually a local company called Cleveland Kraut, which boasts "crafted fermentation." Brother-in-laws Drew Anderson and Luke Visnic decided that Cleveland needed a sauerkraut it would be proud to call its own (and would complement the staple of a Clevelander's diet, that being smoked meat).

The Polish Girl, spicy kielbasa with shaved brisket and cole slaw, was maybe the best sausage I've ever had.

Noodlecat
234 Euclid Ave., 216-589-0007

When it opened, Jonathon Sawyer's Noodlecat was revolutionary, the first noodle house in Cleveland. Their menu is broken down into three sections: noodles, buns, and veggies. Their pitch line is "sip, slurp, repeat, enjoy." Until 2015, over one hundred thousand bowls of ramen were served by Noodlecat in stand F-3 of the West Side Market, but they couldn't come to terms on a lease extension. There is a new location planned for Crocker Park in Westlake, not yet opened as I write.

Pura Vida
170 Euclid Ave., 216-987-0100

Pure Vida is Chef Brandt Evans's Public Square contribution to Cleveland's culinary scene. After a stint in New York's Alva restaurant, he returned home to open his first restaurant, Blue Canyon Kitchen and Tavern, in Twinsburg, Ohio. So far, Chef Brandt's awards don't match Michael Symon's. He's won the lesser known "Top Chef" at St. John West Shore Festival of the Arts (in 2008 and 2009), and he was chosen to be a Chef Ambassador for the Wisconsin Cheese Board (in 2009 and 2010). Doesn't mean his food isn't great.

At Pura Vida you can get your share of meat and chicken, but they also offer a separate vegetarian menu (almost shocking in this town). There's a "chicken-fried" cauliflower with rustic gravy that sounds like a kind of methadone for recovering meat addicts.

Ristorante Chinato
2079 E. 4th St., 216-298-9080

This is Zack Bruell's very upscale Italian restaurant. You don't come here for your spaghetti with meatballs or calzone. Here you can get your stewed squid and clam belly with vegetable fritto misto and lemon mayo, your pappardelle with pecorino and pepperoncini (say that three times fast), or your Bistecca All Fiorentina for two (yeah, I have *no* idea what that is).

Bruell has said, "To create the ideal restaurant, the energy and environment are just as important as the cuisine." For my taste— and thankfully Zack Bruell doesn't know what I look like—the food at Chinato is presented beautifully and tastes magnificent. But the decor looks like what a chef too long in the kitchen might view as elegant. I'd say the Delta Sky Club lounge at the Hopkins Airport has more personality.

Slyman's
3106 St. Clair Ave., 216-621-3760

There's a local story (myth) that people who fly into Cleveland Hopkins Airport first find their luggage and then find Slyman's. The restaurant's been around since 1964, when Lebanese immigrants Joe and Mae Slyman wanted to show thanks for their new freedom with huge sandwiches (not free). The corned beef sandwich currently goes for $14.50. But when you bear witness to the size of it, between 12 and 14 ounces, the dollar-per-ounce ratio is no more than McDonald's Dollar Menu. Their motto is "Quality AND Quantity."

As much as their massive corned beef sandwiches, the atmosphere is the reason to go. Outside are streets that will have you wondering if your car will still be there after lunch.

Inside, son Freddie runs Slyman's today, helped by brother Moe Slyman working the counter and cousin Samir Elnahass slicing the thin-cut beef. The movie *Big Night* comes to mind watching

Slyman's is proud of the quality (and size) of their ingredients
Credit: Michael Murphy

Freddie, Moe, and Samir passionately argue with each other in a way I absolutely loved. It was a joy to watch men who have been faithfully standing in their Slyman's T-shirts and aprons, slicing corned beef for some forty years, and yet are still so passionate about their work.

Slyman's is clearly a spot for regulars. Most incoming customers first stop by the counter to exchange greetings with Freddie and Moe. One massive human being, who looked like he could have played for the Cleveland Browns back when they were good, was led to "his" table. The fifty-something waitresses, one with shockingly large hair dyed shoe-polish black, exchanged banter laced with obvious familiarity and gave flirtatious free back scratches as she slid behind customers.

Esquire magazine chose their corned beef as an "unimpeachable" Best Sandwich in America.

Slyman's opened a new location in Beachwood, by I-271 and nestled among Fairfield Inn and Extended Stay hotels. I ate there too. Everything right about the original was decidedly wrong here. Fifty-year-old lifetime waitresses were replaced by twenty-year-old guys in man buns. Twelve large-screen TVs assaulted your eyes while bad retro rock assaulted your ears. For my money, the sliders were no better than at Applebees.

Sterle's Country House
1401 E. 55th St., 216-881-4181

A landmark since 1954, Sterle's was founded by Frank Sterle, an immigrant from Ljubljana, Slovenia. He started out with a few picnic tables, one waitress, and no menus. They only served a few things, like wiener schnitzel, chicken paprikash, and stuffed cabbage.

Rick Semersky bought the restaurant in 2012 simply to keep the institution open for business. In addition to Old World food, the restaurant offers lively renditions of Old World music. They've had featured polka performances by notable artists Joey

Miskulin, Johnny Vadnal, "Waltz King" Lou Trebar, and the man himself, Frankie Yankovic, a.k.a. "The King of Polka."

OHIO CITY AND TREMONT

I never heard of Ohio City or Tremont before preparing to write this book. The neighborhoods were on the "wrong" side of the Cuyahoga River. For us nose-in-the-air East Clevelanders, anything West of the river was viewed as a vast wasteland of Polka music. We imagined a slower-tempo Polka was played for funerals and church mass.

Ohio City and Tremont today have become the center of the new culinary scene in Cleveland.

Barrio
503 Prospect Ave., 216-862-4652
In the neighborhood now known for late-night joints where you can bury tomorrow's potential hangover in butter and deep-fried remedies, Barrio may be the #1 spot. Here you can mix and match a great variety of queso and other taco ingredients. If you're drunk, the Chorizo Queso is highly recommended. If otherwise imbued, go with the Stoner Quest.

The Black Pig
2801 Bridge Ave., 216-862-7551
The Black Pig, sometimes called just "The Pig," is chef Michael Nowak's vision of hog heaven. Here you can get your pork belly, pork meatballs, pork tenderloin, braised pork collar, smoked pork chop, and chili cheese pork rinds. To break up the meat sweats, you can order sides of roasted Ohio carrots or brussels sprouts. And then get right back on the acute myocardial infarction caravan (maybe I should trademark that phrase before Guy Fieri steals it) with braised short ribs or the Black Pig burger.

Ohio currently ranks twelfth in the country in deaths by cardiovascular disease. Don't blame The Black Pig. It's doing its best to help Cleveland crack the Top 10.

Crop Bistro and Bar
2537 Lorain Ave., 216-696-2767

The most impressive thing about Crop Bistro may be the setting. Housed in a classic 1925 building designed by architects Frank Walker and Harry Weeks, you'll eat in a massive seventeen-thousand-square-foot space, seated next to six massive arched windows, with marble and "faux painted" columns leading up to an intricate coffered ceiling thirty-five feet in the air, bronze light fixtures ornamented in gold, and a massive mural signed by artist Glenn Shaw hanging over a Carrara-marble-topped bar. The location was originally the United Bank Building. The old bank vault serves as a private dining room.

Restaurateur Steve Schimoler is a man with a massive plan. He has established his Crop Restaurant Group with the express intent of expanding his brand across the city. Crop: The Group is modeled after Richard Melman, the founder and CEO of Lettuce Entertain You Enterprises, a Chicago Group with more than one hundred restaurant venues. Schimoler has said Melman "is my restaurant business hero," and that his Crop Group was "stealing a page from the playbook" of the Lettuce Group.

He opened Crop Bistro's first offshoot, Crop Kitchen, which Schimoler positioned as "destined to be our comfort food, our version, comfortable for that demographic." It closed, however, after little more than a year. He's also opened Crop Rocks (reminding me of the terrible cop-musical TV series) and Crop Sticks on the East Bank of the Flats. Crop Kitchen, Crop Rocks, and Crop Sticks are no more, but On Air, which opened in February 2016, remains as of the time of this writing. It combines Caribbean-inspired food with live music. One group that has played there there is Cream of the Crop, featuring Schimoler on drums.

Dante
2247 Professor Ave., 216-274-1200
Dante Boccuzzi also has a group, Dante Dining Group, with restaurants Dante, Dante Next Door (literally next door), Ginko (in the basement of Dante), and Coda (beneath Dante Next Door). It's like a kibbutz of Dante restaurants. There's also Dante's Inferno inside Progressive Field, and Dante Boccuzzi's in Akron, known as DBA.

Fahrenheit
2417 Professor Ave., 216-781-8858
Chef-owner Rocco Whalen here tries (and succeeds) to be all things to all people. As one of Cleveland's top chefs, he is required to master meat. His 18-Hour Ohio Pork Shank rivals any dish served at the city's other carnivorous manors. But he also has a vegetarian menu and Fahren-Lite for calorie-conscious diners. As one who clearly doesn't count calories, I'm a sucker for his bacon-wrapped and chorizo-stuffed dates. Bacon goes with everything. I have read about, but have not eaten, Rocco's sweet potato biscuit with lobster and Neese's sausage gravy. Sounds ridiculously good.

Fat Cats
2061 W. 10th St., 216-579-0200 and Lava Lounge
1307 Auburn Ave., 216-589-9112
While Michael Symon may be the George Washington of Cleveland's restaurant revolution, Ricardo Sandoval might be considered the city's culinary Molly Pitcher—nowhere as well known but still quite important. Sandoval is never mentioned in national food magazines or on TV shows. He has no awards as best chef. He focuses on his ever-changing menu at Fat Cats, served in a

Fat Cats is also a popular weekend brunch spot

shabby-chic converted home tagged as "funky," a "little treasure," and "a gem."

There he serves global small and large plates, dishes like bouillabaisse, seared duck breast, and sausage-and-goat-cheese rigatoni. Sandoval notes, "We change the menu at least four times a year depending on our farmer's availability. We also have an herb and heirloom garden behind the restaurant."

Two years after opening Fat Cats, Sandoval purchased another building located on the south end of Tremont, an area that used to be a bit more sketchy. He converted the former Trotters into Lava

Lounge. "I basically had to make peace with some local criminals so they wouldn't mug my customers."

Serving inexpensive and innovative dishes like tofu steamed buns, chickpea tacos, and apple, cheddar, and pickled brussels sprouts on flatbread, all served into the late hours in a funky location with a trendy second-floor bar, made the Lava Lounge a favorite service-industry hangout, considered one of the coolest places in Cleveland.

Sandoval has more recently opened Felice Urban Cafe (12502 Larchmere Blvd., 216-791-0918). Felice is open in Shaker Heights, but is based in a three-story house and retains his penchant for funky settings and inexpensive but gourmet-level food.

The Flying Fig
2523 Market Ave., 216-241-4243

Since the early 2000s, Alice Waters's passion for organic food has grown to become a full-fledged national revolution of locally sourced and farm-to-table restaurants. While not alone, Karen Small, owner and chef of The Flying Fig, may be Cleveland's most passionate advocate. In addition to running her restaurant, Chef Karen also teaches cooking classes that encourage healthy eating for children and nutritious choices for the financially challenged rather than bargain coupons for Fruity Pebbles and refried beans.

Jack Flap's
3900 Lorain Ave., 216-961-5199

Jack Flap's has two locations. This Ohio City location is their breakfast spot, open 7 a.m. until 2 p.m. The Jack Flap's in the 5th Avenue Arcade is the luncheon spot, open 7 a.m. until 2 p.m. Owner Randy Carter more recently opened a third location called Sammich (651 East 185 St.). Their hours vary, but they're generally open 11 a.m. until 6 p.m.

Restaurant Hospitality magazine, a trade publication, honored his sandwich, which combines Vietnamese sausage, a fried egg, kimchi, house-made hot sauce, and Vietnamese cinnamon, as the best in the country.

Cleveland Scene raves about the house bacon, which they call "the best in town. Pork belly is slow-cooked until it is melt-in-your-mouth tender. It's glazed with a syrupy Mexican Coca-Cola and sliced into fat, smoky slabs that go great with everything on the menu."

Lucky's Cafe
777 Starkweather Ave., 216-622-7773

Most often a line will be camped outside the front door of Lucky's, especially at brunch time. Some of Lucky's notoriety was created by bloviator-host Guy Fieri. "Real" chefs, like Michael Symon, also sing its praise. Simon raved about Lucky's Biscuits and Gravy on the show *The Best Thing I Ever Ate*.

I would put their Caramel Creme Breve on my list as one of the Best Things I Ever Drank. It's made with house-made caramel, espresso, milk, and cream. You should order one just to take a snap of its frothy beauty to post on Facebook or Instagram.

Momocho Mod Mex
1835 Fulton Rd., 216-694-2122

Chef Eric Williams had a considerable hole from which he had to dig out to make it into this book. He won Guy's Grocery Games: Diners, Drive-Ins and Dives Tournament. In case I've been too shy or understated, I hate Guy Fieri. When an anglo guy named Williams tags his restaurant "Autentico" Mexican cuisine, he's digging a deeper hole.

But his considerable talent gets him out. His restaurant is known as much for their margaritas as the food. Many consider their cucumber margarita the best. They also serve hibiscus, red bell pepper, ginger, and blood orange margaritas.

Momocho offers five different salsas and seven types of guacamole (including goat cheese with tomato chile and poblano peppers, jicama with pineapple, chile habanero, mint, and garlic confit with bleu), and thirteen varieties of taquitos.

Williams added El Carnicero, a second Mexican restaurant in a larger space (16918 Detroit Ave., 216-226-3415) to allow him more creativity.

Parallax
2179 W. 11th St., 216-583-9999
Zack Bruell has been called the godfather of fusion cuisine in Cleveland. His professional culinary journey began at the Restaurant School in Philadelphia. Upon graduation, he moved to California and began working under visionary chef Michael McCarty, credited with creating California cuisine. Bruell returned home to Cleveland.

Parallax was an early foundation of what would become his ten-restaurant empire. His others include Chinato (Italian), Cow-

Upscale and sophisticated, Parallax is known for its inventive Asian fusion dishes

ell & Hubbard (French), L'Albatros (French brasserie), Table 45 (global), Dynomite Burgers inside Progressive Field, Alley Cat (a waterfront oyster bar), and more recently, the casual Exploration inside the Cleveland Museum of Natural History.

His trademark style is layering many distinctive flavors into each dish. Each item on the menu reads like a short novella of ingredients. Parallax offers striped bass with green tea noodles, wakame, wild mushrooms, and gari jus; loup de mer with red curry sauce, sticky rice, and green papaya salad; and Alaskan black cod with miso glaze, bamboo rice, and bok choy.

Bruell has been nominated several times for the James Beard Award. The smart money is on him soon enough joining fellow award-winning Cleveland chefs Michael Symon and Jonathon Sawyer.

Prosperity Social Club
1109 Starkweather Ave., 216-937-1938

Any restaurant with "Social Club" in its name portends great things. The Prosperity Social Club delivers on the promise on multiple levels. It is located in a 1938 building that formerly served as a Polish workingman's club. They retained the rustic wood panels, pictures of Warsaw and Gdansk on the walls, and old Blatz and Stilts beer signs behind the bar.

On any given visit, you'll join an eclectic mix of neighborhood locals, pierced and tattooed hipsters, struggling artists, struggling couples trying to make an impression on a first date, and families hunkering down after their kid's soccer or softball game.

The social club is known for Wednesday night, dubbed Old World Wednesdays. On this night, they feature favorites such as Hungarian and Polish stuffed cabbage, kielbasa, ricotta or potato pierogi, and potato pancakes. The food is paired with ethnic beers such as Okocim from Poland and Staropramen Lager from the Czech Republic, and brought to Old World perfection with Stan Mejac playing the accordion from 6 p.m. to 10 p.m.

Prosperity Social Club is equally popular for their Friday fish fry, which they call "Gotta Haddock."

Their beer-battered haddock is served until 2 a.m.

Sherla's Chicken & Oysters
900 Literary Rd., 216-771-5652

When Michael Symon announced in May 2016 he was closing the fire-damaged Lolita and replacing it (in the same spot) with Sherla's Chicken & Oysters, many regulars were apoplectic. They panicked they'd lose their favorite fried chicken. It will be still served at Sherla's. They begged to restore the eggplant dip. Michael says that remains as a seasonal possibility. But Lolita's faithful will have to learn to live without his mac and cheese. Chef says twenty years is enough. Sherla's main focus will be on seafood, especially smoked fish. Oysters will be served raw, wood-grilled, or Rockefeller-style. The restaurant is not yet open as I write, but most likely will be as you read.

Sokolowski's University Inn
1201 University Rd., 216-771-9236

Victoria and Michael Sokolowski opened Sokolowski's University Inn in 1923 as a tavern at the corner of University Road and West 13th Street. They expanded it from bar to lunch spot, serving generous portions of Polish comfort food to neighborhood steel workers. Today, it remains a family business, Cleveland's oldest family-owned restaurant, run by grandchildren Mike, Mary, and Bernie Sokolowski.

They still serve steel workers, but have also become an "in spot" for visiting celebrities like Bill Clinton and Jimmy Fallon. Sokolowski's has appeared on Michael Symon's *The Best Thing I Ever Ate* on the Food Network and Anthony Bourdain's *No Reservations*.

On Fridays, you can replace bratwurst, kielbasa, and pierogi with perch, cod, and scrod. Wednesday through Saturday, your

Family owned since 1923

meal comes with the live sounds of Tom "Mr. T at the Keys" Ballog. If you go, tell me Mr. T at the Keys doesn't look just like Tor Johnson, the old B-Movie star from the 1950s.

In 2014, Sokolowski's won the James Beard "American Classics" Award. It feels exactly like a well-worn classic, with cafeteria-style service and a three-foot-high statue of the Pope on the cafeteria-style counter top.

Outside may be the best view of Cleveland's skyline.

The South Side
2207 W. 11th St., 216-937-2288
Yet another late late-night joint in Tremont. This one serves chicken and waffles any hour of the day or night. They are known as much for their ambiance. South Side has what's considered Cleveland's nicest patio for outdoor seating and, as a nod to Cleveland's winters, a fireplace inside to keep warm while you eat their turkey Cuban sandwich, tacos, flatbreads, or mussel bowls. The

South Side is also back-to-back "Best Bloody Mary" champion of the city.

West Side Market
1979 W. 25th St., 216- 664-3387

After the Terminal Tower and LeBron James's billboard, the West Side Market, with its 137-foot clock tower, is probably the most recognizable sight for locals and tourists. Two prominent businessmen and former mayors of Ohio City, Josiah Barber and Richard Lord, donated land at Lorain Avenue and Pearl Street (later named West 25th Street) to the city for the express purpose of establishing an open-air market. The Pearl Market served the

West Side Market has operated continuously for more than one hundred years

area for seventy-five years. Then, in 1912, the market moved to a larger spot directly across the street. The grand, yellow brick building has one hundred indoor stalls under a stunning forty-four-feet-high Guastavino tile vaulted ceiling and eighty-five outdoor produce stands. Six days a week, the market opens at 7 a.m. The seventh, Sunday, it opens at noon. Tenants, some of which have occupied stalls for multiple generations, peddle food of Irish, German, Slovenian, Italian, Greek, Polish, Russian, and Middle Eastern descent. You'll feel a bit like you're in a crowded Middle Eastern market, but in place of choosing exotic tapestries or spices, your choices will be clothespin cookies or kolacky cookies, and whether to take home beef tongue, beef kidneys, or beef hearts.

In addition to drawing film crews from the *Food Network* and the *Travel Channel*, area chefs, home cooks, and tourists visit the market. They even provide guided tours. A wonderful experience can be had guide-free by taking a somewhat hard to find staircase and just sitting on the second floor to gaze down on the vast expanse of activity.

UNIVERSITY CIRCLE, LITTLE ITALY, SHAKER SQUARE

This was the "classy" area of Cleveland. The Art Museum, Severance Hall (where the world-class orchestra plays), and Case Western Reserve University all line University Circle.

Edwin's Leadership & Restaurant
13101 Shaker Sq., 216-921-3333
What sounds like a place where you'd hear motivational speakers tell you how to get from good to great or to learn who moved your cheese, Edwin's Leadership is an institute that gives formerly incarcerated adults the skills and support to learn the restaurant and hospitality industry. They take in roughly one hundred ex-

cons a year and can boast an astonishing 95 percent employment rate for those who graduate from the program.

And the food is not the rubbery chicken or lukewarm lasagna you'd be served listening to Tony Robbins or Les Brown. Edwin's serves French cuisine such as cuisses de grenouilles en persillade (frog legs), tarte de lapin au parmesan et jambon en route (rabbit), and escargot de bourgogne au fenouil et beurre à l'ail (snails).

The restaurant has received three stars from *The Plain Dealer*, was regarded by *The New York Times* as "High-Stakes Haut Cuisine," is a Silver Spoon winner as Best French restaurant in the city from *Cleveland Magazine*, and was called one of the best new restaurants in Cleveland by both *Cleveland Scene* and Eater.com.

Fire Food & Drink
13220 Shaker Sq., 216-921-3473
Housed in a historic 1929 building, the centerpiece is the open kitchen, where you can watch your meal be prepared, or not.

Chef Katz, nominated for the James Beard Award in 2014, is very involved in the community. He is a national and international advocate for food that is sustainable, healthful, and local. He is a former president of Cleveland Independents, an organization that nurtures and promotes local independent restaurants. And he goes out of his way to credit local farmers for the food he serves.

Happy Dog at the Euclid Tavern
11625 Euclid Ave., 216-231-5400
The Euclid Tavern, a.k.a. the Euc, will be more fully profiled in the Nightlife chapter. Here, it is included for its hot dogs rather than its musical acts. The Euc was an institution during its long history from 1909 until it closed in 2013, then reopened under the auspices and energy of Happy Dog.

L'Albatros
11401 Bellflower Rd., 216-791-7880

Zack Bruell's French bistro. It is supposedly pronounced "LAL-bah-trow." While the entrées are the main event, L'Albatros is also known for their assiettes de fromage (cheese plates) and cozy outdoor settings.

Michaelangelo's
2198 Murray Hill Rd., 216-721-0300

Chef Michael Annandono's Italian cuisine served in Little Italy. But, in place of mounds of pasta and red sauce, the restaurant offers the less obvious prosciutto-wrapped wild boar chops, homemade veal-stuffed cannelloni, and tagliolini in a ragout of duck, veal, and guinea fowl. Muscovy duck breast, roasted rosy with orange, is considered Annandono's signature dish.

Nora
2181 Murray Hill Rd., 216-231-5977

Another Little Italy landmark. This newish restaurant calls itself "Italian Food Reinvented." Chef Eddie Zalar tweaks traditional spaghetti, serving his with middleneck clams, chicken chorizo, Nora marinara, smoked cherry tomatoes, and pickled apples. The ravioli choices aren't meat, mushroom, or cheese, but duck confit, artichoke puree, peas, preserved lemon, mint, and toasted hazelnuts.

Tommy's
1824 Coventry Rd., 216-321-7757

Attached to Mac's Backs Bookstore and two doors down from Big Fun, Tommy's is, like them, a Coventry institution. I had overlooked Tommy's in my first draft until Big Fun's Steve Presser took me there for lunch.

Opening in 1972, Tommy's was one of Cleveland's first v̶ tarian restaurants. Vegetarianism actually goes back to ·

Greece and Pythagoras. Ben Franklin was a vegetarian. John Harvey Kellogg, creator of cornflakes and king of the cereal empire, was a strong advocate of vegetarianism and preached its benefits in the 1940s. The American Vegetarian Party formed in hopes of electing a president in 1948.

Tommy's has almost as much history. Harvey Pekar ate there as his regular place. SNL cast member Molly Shannon was a waitress there. In addition to their famous wraps, falafel, variety of salads, and spinach pies, they do serve meat. As claimed on their website, "Whether you're a vegetarian, a meat-eater, vegan, or just plain hungry, Tommy will take care of you!"

They are as famous, maybe more famous, for their twenty-ounce shakes. Their chocolate shake has 680 calories. *Rolling Stone* magazine voted Tommy's the "Best Milkshake East of the Mississippi." *Cleveland Scene* wrote, "Don't even attempt to use a straw to sip these monsters." Steve Presser taught me how to pour one from the stainless steal mixing cup into your glass. It is an art more subtle and complex than getting ketchup from a Heinz 57 bottle. I would advise you to save a dry cleaning bill and let your experienced waitress do her job.

Trentina
1903 Ford Dr., 216-421-2900
Trentina's is James Beard Award–winning chef Jonathon Sawyer's take on Italian cuisine. Only rather than expected pasta, his menu showcases the distinct cuisine of the Tyrolean region, which is equally inspired by Germany and France. The results are dishes like Gnocchetti Sardi (osso bucco–style Ohio beef on top of Sardinian noodles in a charred herb crema with dehydrated olive), Confit Duck (maple-glazed duck leg served with shagbark seed and mill polenta and roasted farm carrots), and the fish of the day grilled over live fire with chive soubise, roasted potato, and olive tapenade. Trentina also offer a twelve-course tasting menu called Menu Bianco.

ment. He started with a small storefront in Lakewood and has now grown to seven full-service locations and three quick-service ones. Other locations are Melt Cafe at 200 Public Square, 13463 Cedar Road in Cleveland Heights, 6700 Rockside Road in Independence, plus Mentor, and Akron, and two in Columbus, Ohio.

Pier W

12700 Lake Ave., 216-228-2250

Dining at Pier W is like an adventure ride. You don't even see the restaurant as you park your car. Entering at ground level, the restaurant is actually beneath you. You descend in a glass elevator through a sleek lounge, and only then you see the payoff, a spectacular view of Cleveland's skyline. The restaurant is designed to resemble a luxury liner seemingly crashed into a cliff above Lake Erie.

Pier W is considered one of the city's best seafood restaurants. You can taste a broad spectrum by ordering their iced seafood tower (jumbo gulf shrimp, poached lobster, selected oysters, chilled mussels, lump crab salad). They are also known as one of Cleveland's best brunch spots, as verified by their making Open-Table's national 2016 list of Best US Brunch Restaurants.

JUST OUTSIDE THE CITY PROPER

B Spot Burgers

18066 Royalton Rd., in Strongsville, 440-572-9600

B Spot is Michael Symon's burger joint, plus his other favorite B-foods; bologna, brats, and beer. B Spot is the four-time SOBEWFF Burger Bash champ.

I looked it up, SOBEWFF. It's the South Beach Wine and Food Festival. I guess Michael Symon didn't take the same shit from locals as LeBron did when he took *his* talents to South Beach.

WORLD CUISINE

Krishnendu Ray wrote an entire book, *The Ethnic Restaurateur*, pointing out the inappropriateness of the term "ethnic food." So, I'll try to avoid it.

Italian, Mexican, and Chinese food you can get in Anytown, USA. Polish, Hungarian, Slovenian, and meat-rich cuisines are very much a Cleveland thing. But the city also has a number of excellent restaurants for other nationalities.

Algebra Tea House
2136 Murray Hill Rd., 216-421-9007
Ayman Alkayali, a Palestinian refugee who came to Cleveland to study at Case Western Reserve University, created the tea house as a place for discussions and dining on his much-missed home food: Iraqi kebabs, Damascus eggplant, Moroccan stew, and shakshouka.

Anatolia Cafe
2270 Lee Rd., 216-321-4400
Yashar Yildirim opened his pioneering Anatolia Cafe in 2007. Dining either inside or the sidewalk patio, they serve authentic Turkish and Mediterranean dishes. In addition to thin-sliced doner kebabs, a mixture of lamb and beef, with tavuk adana, grilled ground chicken, yogurt, Anatolia also offers Turkish wines.

Caribe Bake Shop
2906 Fulton Rd., 216-281-8194
Caribe serves Puerto Rican baked goods and simple sandwiches and carries essential grocery items. Their hot food selections include pinto bean stew with roast pork or steak options. Sweet plantains go with everything.

Frank's Falafel House

1823 W. 65th St., 216-631-3300

Pretty sure this is not the same Frank of Frank's Seafood. In addition to falafel, Frank's serves other traditional Middle Eastern dishes such as shish tawook, marinated chicken in a garlic sauce, and shawarma, seasoned beef served in a wrap with tahini sauce and tabbouleh.

Pupuseria La Bendicion

3685 W. 105th St., 216-688-0338

This Salvadorian restaurant makes the best pupusa in Cleveland, maybe the entire state of Ohio. It is quite likely that Pupuseria La Bendicion is the only Salvadorian restaurant in Ohio.

Rumi's Market and Deli

8225 Carnegie Ave., 216-229-7864

Rumi's is primarily an international food market and bakery, but they do have a food court for Middle Eastern and North African "fast" food.

Seoul Hot Pot

3709 Payne Ave., 216-881-1221

Owners Jin and Bok Hu emigrated from Seoul with their three children back in 1983. With the goal to live out the American dream, the Hus first opened DeAngelo's Pizza in 1985.

"We discovered it wasn't working, and everyone who came in wanted our Korean food."

Superior Pho, a.k.a. Pho Hoa

3211 Payne Ave., 216-781-7462

There are now several Vietnamese restaurants in Cleveland. Superior Pho was the first and remains the best.

★ ★ ★

Having profiled Cleveland's star chefs, food festivals, signature mustard, and popcorn balls in the previous chapter, plus forty-some Cleveland restaurants in this one, I'm still not done. Cleveland, built by the Polish, Czechs, Hungarians, and Slovenes, was and is a carnivore's paradise. You can't thoroughly discuss Cleveland's food culture without including its butchers.

Butcher & Brewer (2043 E. 4th St.) was voted best new restaurant by *Cleveland Scene* when they opened in 2014. The brewpub is known for both beer and brats, with a staff of an in-house butcher and charcutier. The city's premier food writer, Douglas Trattner, honored them as "the most ambitious, audacious, and daring dining project to land in Cleveland."

For my elitist taste, I favor Old World butchers, with employees wearing blood- and gristle-smeared aprons and that have been around since the Earth first cooled.

Azman & Sons Market fits my bill. They have been at the same location since 1924 (6501 St. Clair Ave.). The Azman family first began working in the sausage business in their Slovenia village of Ig. That's right, Ig. They immigrated to America during World War I and settled amidst the largest Slovenian community in the country. Current third-generation owner Frank Azman III has been working meats for the past four decades. He credits the butcher's long success to their customer service and commitment to the community. In one instance, they displayed their community commitment by letting a beauty pageant queen ride waving from the back of their emergency back-up Model T after she missed her parade float.

Frank III argues against these new whippersnapper stainless-steel smokehouses, preferring the flavor of sausage slowly smoked over cherry wood in his brick smokehouse.

The Sausage Shop (4501 Memphis Ave.) dates back to 1938. They serve a variety of sausage, bratwurst, wieners, chops, loins, and other meats, many using the same recipes that were originally brought to Cleveland from Schewinfurt, Germany. Their Holiday Kielbasa is a mix of beef and pork, with mustard seed, garlic, and a sweet sauterne white wine.

Gibbs Butcher Block (9858 E. River Rd., Columbia Station) has been around "only" since the 1950s, though their building is one hundred years older. They make over two hundred varieties of sausage, but merely present thirty-five different kinds at any one time. "We really don't make any traditional sausages," says owner Jim Dixon. "We like to mix things up" by serving items like an apple bacon pumpkin sausage. Every Saturday from noon to 4 p.m., the store grills up sausages for free tastings.

Raddell's Sausage Shop (478 E. 152nd St.) is a fourth-generation, family-owned Slovenian sausage shop best known for their award winning smoked Slovenian sausage, which won the Polka Hall-of-Fame People's Choice Award four years in a row.

K&K Meat Shoppe (6172 Dunham Rd., in Maple Heights) is a newbie, opened in 1979, but employs three generations of meat cutters. K&K offers award-winning Polish kielbasa, as featured in *Cleveland Magazine*, smoked Polish, Hungarian, and Slovenian sausage, hurka, jaternice, kizka, spec/sulana, paprika bacon, Bohemian wieners, and homemade Bohemian sekanice. On Thursdays, they feature their roasted pork with homemade spaetzle. The fact that you need to google hurka, jaternice, kizka, sekanice, and spaetzle to understand this paragraph hopefully makes K&K all the more inviting.

There's also **Tibor's Kosher Meats** (2185 S. Green Rd.), **TJ's Butcher Block and Deli** (14415 Detroit Ave.), **State Meats** (5338 State Rd.), and **Vince's Meats** (inside the West Side Market, 1979 W. 25th St.). And there are seemingly new premier butchers opening every half-year. Melissa Khoury walked away from her job as executive chef of Washington Place Bistro to open **Saucisson**, a boutique butchery offering fresh and cured meats and sausages. Adam Lambert (not the *American Idol* star) left as executive chef at Bar Cento to open the **Meat & Curing Co.**, a retail butcher shop focusing on fresh cuts of meat, house-roasted deli meats and charcuterie.

The dziadek (Polish for grandfather) of Cleveland butchers is **Jaworski Meats** (7545 Pearl Road in Middleburg Heights). Fred Jaworski opened up a small butcher in the Slavic neighborhood of the old Newburgh Market. Fred was known simply as "The Kielbasa King."

Back in the day, Polish meat markets dotted Broadway and Fleet, then the largest concentration of Poles in the region. The butchers are all gone now, sacrifices to suburban flight and the rise of supermarkets. Jaworski Meats survived seventy years, but then about ten years ago, they moved to Middleburg Heights, a less hardscrabble community.

Fred's son, Mark Jaworski, runs the butcher shop today. You can most often find him tucked away in the back, tending to ovens and stoves. Mark's nephew, Adam, works full-time at the market, and mother Dorothy is still going strong, working elbow-deep in ground pork making Kielbasa in their ancient, cranky mixer.

Keeping with tradition, they continue to offer kishka, the Eastern European blood sausage made from "head meat," buckwheat, and barley; sekanice, a special Slovenian ham loaf; as well as kielbasa loaf, stuffed cabbage, and a dozen soups, including oxtail and dill pickle soup, plus czernina, a soup made with duck blood that I hear is delicious. Sorry, I'm not trying it.

OK, *now* we're done with The Food of The Land.

CHAPTER FOUR

The Sporting Life

TITLE TOWN . . . EVERY FIFTY YEARS (GIVE OR TAKE)

This just in: Beverly Hills 90210, Cleveland Browns 3.

—*Colin Mochrie*

ANY CITIES LOVE THEIR SPORTS TEAMS. CHICAGO LOVES DA Bears, and all 650,000 residents of Seattle seem to be the 12th Man for the Seahawks. Boston splits their love among the habitually cheating Patriots, the once dominant and now more unassuming Celtics, and the baseball Sawks. But no city seems anymore aligned with and defined by their sports teams than Cleveland. In this case, until Monday, June 19th, 2016, that wasn't necessarily a good thing.

Forbes magazine in an early 2016 article ranked Cleveland as the #2 worst sports city. They had Buffalo as #1. At the time, I begged to differ. Buffalo at least made it to four Super Bowls, even if they lost all four.

The last fifty-two years (and counting) have been pain-producing football. There are local t-shirts worn by current Browns fans imprinted "Rebuilding Since 1964." Comedian Mike Polk Jr. christened their new stadium "the Factory of Sadness." You can buy T-shirts imprinted with that slogan. Polk also made a video in which he responded to the Browns season ticket office, suggesting a new payment plan. He wished to decline purchasing tickets for the final two home games because he's noticed that tickets for final games each year can be purchased for $6 on StubHub or as little as two menthol cigarettes from a scalper outside the stadium.

Another fan posted an ad on Craigslist:

Have you played pro football? College ball? High school? Pee-wee?

Have you played Madden before?

Do you sort of kind of know some of the rules of football?

We can teach you the basics ... throwing the ball to the guy who has the same color shirt as you. Throwing the ball more than 3 yards on 3rd and 16. Come on down! You're the next contestant on Cleveland Quarterbacks!

For that perfect gift, you can buy *Why Is Daddy Sad on Sunday: Disappointing Moments in Cleveland Sports Coloring Book*, which contains twenty-five line drawings depicting scenes of Cleveland's biggest sports letdowns. My reaction was, "Only twenty-five?"

However, in spite of our self-effacing humor, I and other Browns fans get outraged when under-forty-year-old sports "experts" and pundits roll out their tired lists of greatest quarterbacks of all time or greatest football teams ever, and they always leave Otto Graham and the Browns of the 1940s and '50s off the list. Otto Graham played ten years and took the Browns to nine championships, winning seven. Their record over those ten years was 140-20. The Browns were pro football champions in 1946, '47, '48, '49, '50, '54, '55, and '64. They also played in the title game in 1951, '52, '53, '57, and '65.

For readers mathematically challenged, that's thirteen championship appearances in a twenty-year stretch. Only the Boston

Celtics and UConn women's basketball can rival that legacy. Otto and the Browns's accomplishments leave in the dust Joe Montana's 49ers and Tom Brady's Deflatriots. Just because these "experts" weren't around to see it doesn't mean it didn't happen.

Admittedly, this was an era when teams were for the most part put together with slow-footed white guys whose off-season regimens consisted of guzzling beer and brats rather than masking HGH, but you deal with the reality of the times.

My father used to tell anyone who'd listen that he once held every single passing record for Lincoln Ferndale High in Detroit. He wasn't lying either. He just failed to mention he was the first person to ever throw a forward pass back in the days of the single wing. Every time he threw the football, it was a new record.

I worry if I went back here and retold the glory days of Marion Motley, Mac Speedie, and Lou "The Toe" Groza, I would lose every reader except a few old guys huddled over Happy Dogs and a Pilsner at the Euclid Tavern, a.k.a. the Euc.

So let's start with the Browns most recent shining moment . . . December 27, 1964. I was there, Section 6, Row V, Seat #19. My seat probably now sits at the bottom of Lake Erie. When Cleveland tore down the old Municipal Stadium, they used much of the rubble to serve as a breaker wall in the lake to keep stronger waves from hitting the city's shoreline.

Playing the heavily favored Baltimore Colts, the halftime score was 0-0. Famed sports journalist Red Smith wrote, "Never had so many paid so much to see so little." In the second half, quarterback Frank Ryan, with a PhD in Mathematics from Rice University and who was later to be a professor at Yale, connected with Gary Collins for three touchdowns. The ageless Lou "The Toe" kicked two field goals, and the Browns defense continued to baffle the great Johnny Unitas to pull off a lopsided and shocking 27-0 win.

The week prior to the game, *Sports Illustrated* tagged the Browns as "The Laugh Champs" for winning the far inferior

Eastern Division of the NFL. The Baltimore Colts were so confident, their team band serenaded the Browns players with "Taps" as they left their hotel to go play the game.

The play of the game occurred in the first half when All-Pro Johnny Unitas threw a swing pass to All-Pro Lenny Moore. There was nothing but mud painted to look like grass (it was December—in Cleveland) and only one player, Galen Fiss, between Moore and the end zone. Fiss shot into the backfield and took out Moore like a bowling pin for a five yard loss. For me, and probably me alone, it was the greatest play in NFL history. Galen Fiss was my childhood hero. A cut-out picture of Fiss was Elmer's-Glued to the front of my grade-school notebook. When we got home from the game, I could look at an autographed photo of Fiss on my bedroom night stand.

Since 1964, Browns fans have been subjected to heartbreaking losses which have yielded to soul sucking ineptitude. I was only ten years old when the Browns won the NFL Championship. I was of an age that I then believed the team was destined to win and would win forevermore. The next year, when they lost the championship to Green Bay, I felt forsaken by the gods. The gods' betrayal got so much worse a half-year later when Jimmy Brown quit football to finish filming the movie *The Dirty Dozen*. Jim Brown retired after only nine seasons in the NFL.

At the time of Brown's retirement, he held every record. He was the NFL's MVP the very year he quit. He was only twenty-nine years old. Had he played more seasons, there's little doubt his records would still stand today. He is, in my mind, the greatest football player who ever lived. It's not even a debate.

I would go further to claim Jim Brown is one of the greatest two or three athletes of all time. In addition to football, Jim Brown had been an All-American in lacrosse. Some say he is the greatest lacrosse player who ever lived. He also lettered two years at Syracuse in basketball, where he was the second-highest scorer on the team, and track, where Jim Brown was good enough to qualify for the 1956 Olympics in the Decathlon. He chose to focus on football rather than join the American team in Melbourne.

I do recognize "greatest ever" tags are often given to the athlete who wowed you as a deeply impressionable ten year old. For my father, the greatest ever was Bronko Nagurski of his then-hometown Chicago Bears. Besides having the best name in NFL history, Bronko Nagurski has one of the best stories. After running over would-be tacklers, Nagurski knocked himself out cold when he ran into the brick wall at the back of the end zone in Wrigley Field. When he came to, he asked, "Who *was* that last guy who hit me?"

If I had to choose a more recent Browns "hero" it'd probably be Bob Golic. In high school, Bob was a two-sport athlete, perhaps even better at wrestling than football. As a senior at St. Joseph High in Cleveland, he won the Ohio high school heavyweight wrestling championship, beating the previous year's state champ, the undefeated Harold Smith. Smith would go on to be an Olympian.

Pretty much every college in the Midwest, plus Alabama, came after Golic to attend their institutions of higher turnover ratios. He chose Notre Dame, where he played with Joe Montana on the 1977 national champions, and on the 1976 team where Rudy Ruettiger played a total of three plays that became a two hour movie, *Rudy*. Golic belies the movie's claim that Rudy was the first Notre Dame player carried off the field. Golic says he was carried off the field a bunch of times, usually on a stretcher.

The Patriots drafted him as a linebacker. Then he was traded to his hometown Browns, where they converted him into a nose tackle. Forced to gain forty pounds to play the new position, he used his self-described regimen of "Twinkies and a lot of beer."

The new position served him well. He was the All-Pro nose tackle in 1985 and '86, plus a Pro-Bowl player in '87. Golic played six seasons with the Browns, 1982–88, or what some might cruelly call "The Elway Years."

As a player, Golic seemed to love the camera as much as it loved him. He said of himself that he's addicted to being a ham, then adding, "and they haven't found a cure for it, so I guess I'm an uncured ham." Ba-daa-bump.

He turned his fifteen minutes of postgame fame into longer takes as a guest star on the TV show *Coach, Dave's World*, and a recurring role as the dorm advisor on *Saved By the Bell: The College Years*.

Golic has tried a few stints as football commentator, but he was never a good fit for the buttoned-down world that's absorbed Phil Simms and Troy Aikman. One critic said "Golic can be insightful, but he often looks like he'd slept in his clothes, wrestled with his dogs and then played in a flag football game before going on camera."

He now hosts a show on an Akron radio station. I was never able to reach Bob Golic writing this book. That's probably a good thing. He might have punched me harder than he once did Screech on *Saved By the Bell*. I want to know what it feels like to be currently in relative obscurity in Akron while his younger and far less talented brother (both as a football player and as an announcer) has the national ESPN show, *Mike & Mike*, plus endorsement contracts with Dr. Pepper, Nutrisystem, Tabasco hot sauce, and Smithfield Foods.

I have always found Bob Golic charming and irreverent, while I've described Mike Golic as the total opposite.

Of the most recent Browns seasons (i.e., the last FIVE decades), you can make a full-grown Clevelander cry by mentioning the words "Red Right 88," "The Drive," or "The Fumble."

Red Right 88 was the play called at the end of the 1981 AFC Championship. Playing in horrible weather conditions (-16 degrees and a strong wind that had already thwarted two normally makeable field goals), the Browns called a pass play with under two minutes to play and thirteen yards from a victory that would send them to the Super Bowl. Coach Sam Rutigliano told his quarterback, Brian Sipe, "throw it into Lake Erie if the play is anything less than wide open." Instead, Sipe tried to force the ball to Ozzie Newsome and it was picked off by a Raider to preserve their 14-12 win.

The home-team Browns fans watched in horror as John Elway stole the 1986 AFC Championship with a ninety-eight yard, fifteen-play drive to tie the game with thirty-seven seconds left to play. It would simply be known as "The Drive." The Broncos would win in overtime, once again denying the Browns the chance to play in the Super Bowl.

The very next year, this time in Denver, the Browns battled back from a halftime deficit of 3-21. Bernie Kosar led the Browns all the way back to the brink of their first Super Bowl. With a minute left in the game, running back Earnest Byner leaped into the end zone for an apparent go-ahead touchdown . . . except, the ball had been punched out of his hand at the one-foot line and recovered by Denver. It would simply be known as "The Fumble." The Broncos won 38-33. The Browns would never be so close to sniffing a championship again. To this day, I have to flip the TV channel or leave the room if The Drive or The Fumble show up on ESPN Classics.

There is no equally well-worn phrase for when owner Art Modell moved the Browns to Baltimore in 1996. Some call it "The Move." Others say "The Betrayal." In a squabble with the city, Modell signed a lease with Baltimore before Cleveland had a chance to vote and pass the funding of a new stadium (which they did). Many lawsuits between Art Modell and the city of Cleveland followed, including a Congressional hearing. Eventually, Modell was allowed to move his team, but he had to leave the Browns team name and team records back in Cleveland, where an expansion franchise would start play in 1999.

The newly named Baltimore Ravens have won two Super Bowls. The new old Browns, which I call an Elvis Impersonation of the Browns, have become unquestionably the sorriest franchise in the NFL. The year before "The Betrayal," the Browns had gone 11-5 under head coach Bill Belichick and defensive coordinator Nick Saban. Think about that last sentence for a moment and let sink in what might have been.

The Elvis Impersonation Browns now play at FirstEnergy Stadium (100 Alfred Lerner Way). Their first game there on September 12, 1999, saw the Steelers squeak by the Browns 43-0. Since '99, the Browns have had nine head coaches (none with a winning record), twenty-six starting quarterbacks, and a total record of 88-200. In 2016, they were a missed field goal by San Diego kicker Josh Lambo from tying an unbreakable 0-16 season record. You're welcome, Detroit. Maybe FirstEnergy Stadium should be renamed Lambo Field. They have had one playoff appearance, a Wild Card game in 2002. They lost.

If you created a list of the All-Time Biggest Busts of the NFL, it would be loaded with players drafted by the Elvis Impersonation Browns. Courtney Brown, the "can't miss" overall #1 pick in 2000, missed. Gerard Warren was the #3 overall in 2001. He lasted three seasons. Kamerion Wimbley and Barkevious Mingo would solidify the worst-ever defense. The worst-ever offense would be anchored by center Jeff Faine, joined by tight end Kellen Winslow Jr. (sort of a sports version of Frank Sinatra JUNIOR), and wideout Braylon Edwards, a #3 overall pick in the 2005 draft. Edwards hung around for four years, snagging more speeding tickets and assault charges than catches. In the backfield, the worst-ever offense has William Green, an overall #16 NFL pick, and Trent Richardson, #3 overall in 2012. William Green had an injury-riddled career. One injury was being stabbed by his fiancée. Trent Richardson exploded onto the scene in Cleveland— with arthroscopic knee surgery. He played a total of seventeen games with the Browns.

But where the Elvis Impersonation Browns really shine is heretofore unmatched ineptitude at quarterback. Tim Couch was another "can't miss" overall #1 pick. Although Wikipedia

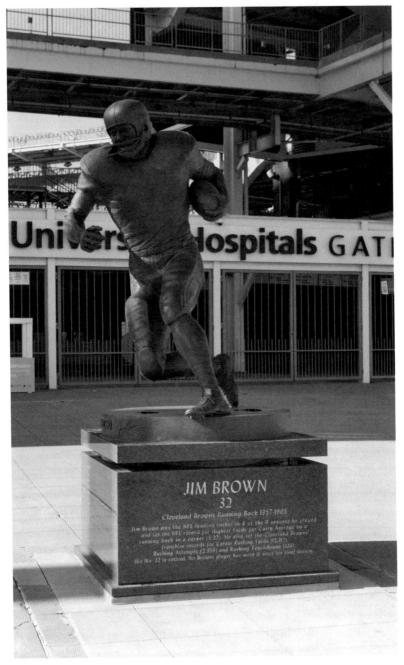

Jim Brown was honored in 2016 with this statue in FirstEnergy Stadium

describes him as the Browns' all-time leader in pass completion at 59.8 percent, many consider the highlight of his five-year career to have been marrying Playmate of the Year Heather Kozar. Brady Quinn, after completing a record-setting career at Notre Dame and winning the Johnny Unitas Golden Arm Award, was a first-round pick by the Browns and thereafter displayed an arm more tin foil than gold. He started a total of twelve games before bouncing around to six other teams. When picked by the Browns, Brandon Weeden became the oldest player chosen in the first round in the history of the NFL. His opening game ended with four interceptions and a passer rating of 5.1. I didn't know the ratings could go into single digits. The game was a portent of things to come. Browns fans brought doctored gallons from garden centers to games. They read, "Weeden Be Gone." Then, Johnny Manziel. Need I say more?

My most memorable play of the post '99 era was executed by a non-player, Paul Serbu. After Art Modell's death in 2012, Serbu traveled from his home in Franklin, Ohio, to Baltimore to record a YouTube video of himself pissing on Modell's grave. Serbu avoided a two-year prison sentence by agreeing to a court-ordered appearance on Modell's son's radio program and apologizing on air.

I seriously doubt the Browns will ever make it to the Super Bowl in my lifetime. When a longtime Browns fan, Scott Entsminger, died in 2013, he requested six players serve as his pallbearers so the Browns could let him down one last time.

As I write, they are set at left tackle with perennial Pro-Bowl pick Joe Thomas. Current pundits and experts claim that after Tom Brady, Joe Thomas is the biggest lock to make the Hall of Fame. But after Thomas, everywhere else the team is built upon a cracked foundation and termite-infested wood. They seem at least a good four or five years from even being competitive, and that's only if they buck trend and start making sound decisions.

The biggest problems are at the top of the organization. Most recently, in addition to hiring another new coach, Hue Jackson, and bringing in another new quarterback, Robert Griffin III—a once promising, then mangled and maligned back-up for the Redskins (who lasted one week before becoming the mangled and sidelined Browns QB)—they've gone in a totally new direction. Some would say they're being innovative, others would say idiotic. They hired Paul DePodesta, a sabermetrics guru from baseball as the chief strategy officer for their dysfunctional football team. Hiring a baseball stats boy to run your football operation is a high-concept move. Sometimes high concepts, like Richard Linklater's *Boyhood*, work out. Sometimes they turn out like Stephen Bochco's *Cop Rock*, the TV musical police drama that lasted eleven episodes.

Upfront, DePodesta feels more like Cop Rock. He did oversee the Dodgers's first playoff win in 16 years, but the next year, they had their worst season in over a decade. After that, he worked with the Padres for three seasons, followed by one season with the Mets, without any great results. Seemingly, he'll fit right in with the Elvis Impersonation Browns. The new Hue Jackson–Paul DePodesta era closed their first season together with a record of 1-15. Their one win came on Christmas Eve. It was Cleveland's version of *Miracle on 34th Street* or *It's a Wonderful Life* (with a sprinkle of *Les Miserables*).

A long-anticipated, at times thought to be just fabled, 30 For 30 documentary aired on ESPN in 2016. *Believeland* is a movie about the long-suffering Cleveland sports fans. The project was started years earlier by director Kristopher Belman, an Akron native. *Believeland* was supposed to air in 2014, the fiftieth anniversary of the last sports championship in Cleveland. When the year came and went, *Believeland* seemed to be just another disappointment. Then, the project got a reboot from another Ohio native filmmaker, Andy Billman.

The film, which interviews fans and players, finally aired on March 31, 2016. A poignant highlight of the movie is ex-Brown Earnest Byner of "The Fumble" starring directly into the camera and saying, "I messed up for everybody. . . . I'm sorry for letting you down."

The baseball Indians over the years have been less heartbreakers than the Browns because their fans often came into each season with extremely low expectations. When I was growing up, the joke (and only slight exaggeration) was that the Indians would be mathematically eliminated each year by June.

The Indians did have some earlier success. It took the suspension of eight Chicago White Sox players for the Indians to eke out the pennant in 1920, but they did go on to win their first World Series against the Brooklyn Dodgers. That World Series had the first ever grand slam, the first home run by a pitcher, and what still stands as the only triple play in World Series history.

For perspective, the Indians' first championship was a month after women won the right to vote in the United States. The Indians won again and for the last time twenty-eight years later in 1948. In 1954, they won more games than any team in baseball history only to be swept by the Giants in the World Series. They more recently were in Game 7 of the World Series and three outs away from a championship in 1997 when Joey Mesa blew the save and the Indians lost to the Marlins in extra innings. Again, in 2016, the Indians made it to a magical Game 7 and took it into extra innings before the Chicago Cubs erased their longest drought without a championship, 108 years. That longest drought now belongs to the Indians.

The Indians probably could have had more success, but the city chased away Clevelander George Steinbrenner the same way they had the auto and aeronautics industries and John D. Rockefeller. Steinbrenner formed a group of local investors to buy the Indians from Vernon Stouffer. The asking price was $10 million. After reviewing the books, the group offered $8 million. Yet Stouffer was adamant; he wanted $10 million. Making no sense, Stouffer rebuffed Steinbrenner's $8 million and later sold the Indians to Nick Mileti, a flashy local promoter, for $1 million in cash and a lot of empty promises.

Steinbrenner bought the Yankees for the same $8 million he offered for the Indians. Under "The Boss" the Yankees went to eleven World Series, winning seven.

I attended my first Indians games in the '60s, when the teams were mired in annual awfulness. When they had a great player, like home run leader Rocky Colavito, or a strikeout king like pitcher Sudden Sam McDowell, they'd trade them away. The entire city went into a funk when Rocky Colavito was traded. He not only hit for power, but had the movie star good looks of Tyrone Power. Pretty much every boy and girl in town wanted to either be him or date him. The Rock had a distinctive warm-up style in the batter's circle where he would twist the bat behind his back from above the shoulders down to his waist. Every Little League and pick-up game all over town would see kids copying Rocky's behind the back moves before they came to bat.

The most memorable moments for the Indians were not walk-off home runs or perfect games, but things like the time lead-off hitter Vic Davalillo fouled off sixteen pitches in one at bat.

I was not in attendance the night of June 4, 1974, the infamous Ten Cent Beer Night. Some promoter for the Cleveland Indians thought it'd be a good idea to sell ten beers for a buck . . . to night-time baseball fans . . . in Cleveland . . . where some guys get into bar fights just for something to do. The game featured a woman running out to the Indians' on-deck circle and flashing her breasts, a naked man sprinting onto the field, and a father-and-son pair jumping into the outfield and mooning the fans in the bleachers. This was all a prelude to a full-scale riot, with drunken fans swarming onto the field with knives, chains, and portions of stadium seats that they had torn apart. The game was called by the umpires, a forfeit loss for the hometown Indians.

I used to love to go to Indians games for the perverse pleasure of watching a game in a seemingly empty stadium. The Indians then shared Municipal Stadium with the Browns. Seating capacity was eighty-five thousand and felt utterly empty when only seven or eight thousand others came to see the last-place baseball team. Yet, the ushers would still chase you out of the completely empty box seats.

For my return trip to Cleveland, I went to Jason "Dirtbag" Kipnis bobblehead night. The second baseman got his nickname because his uniform is always the dirtiest on the field from head-first slides and awkward tumbles around second base. Dirtbag is kind of a perfect player to represent Cleveland. He's always been considered undersized and lacking in major league talent, which he makes up for in grit—one scout called him "pesky."

More than Midwestern grit, Kipnis embodies Cleveland weirdness. Standing at second base, he sings Adele songs, reportedly quite poorly. He also has this bizarre, now-trademarked batting stance.

Dirtbag has said of his stance, "I know it looks stupid. But I'd rather look stupid and dumb standing on the field than really cool in the dugout."

Any discussion or profile of the Indians has to, at some point, deal with Chief Wahoo, called "the most racist mascot in sports." The grinning Indian logo was first drawn by cartoonist Fred George Reinert on the front page of *The Plain Dealer* in 1932. A revised, even more racist, version was created by Walter Goldbach, then a seventeen-year-old. Indians owner Bill Veeck wanted a mascot to "convey a spirit of pure joy and unbridled enthusiasm."

As this book was going to press, Major League Baseball announced that the Cleveland Indians will stop using the Chief Wahoo logo on their jerseys beginning in 2019.

Prior to the Indians' decades of ineptitude, Cleveland had the worst baseball team in history, the 1899 Cleveland Spiders. They were so bad, games drew fewer than two hundred fans per game. Opposing teams eventually refused to come to Cleveland because ticket sales wouldn't offset their travel expenses. The Spiders final 20-134 record remains the all-time worst.

The Cleveland Crunch, a pro soccer team, is an exception to other sports woes. They won three of their six championship appearances in the National Professional Soccer League (NPSL). The league disbanded in 2001. Somehow a championship in a disbanded league for a sport American fans seem to care about (a little) every four years seems not to count.

The Lake Erie Monsters, a professional hockey team in the American Hockey League (AHL), swept the Hershey Bears for the 2016 Calder Cup. Again, second-tier ice hockey, in a country where I doubt many readers can name last year's NHL champion, doesn't seem to count.

Cleveland resident and UFC heavyweight champion Stipe Miocic claimed that when he knocked out Fabricio Werdum he had stopped the curse for Cleveland. As a blue-collar Croatian fireman, he definitely represents for Cleveland. But the fact that you've never heard of Stipe Miocic and probably don't know how to pronounce his name (It's "Steep-A", not "St-IPE") I sense belies his claim of ending the curse. But you can buy Stipe Miocic T-shirts from CLE Clothing Co. (www.clecloth ingco.com).

The city has one other recent champion. Colin Beckford, then a fifteen-year-old junior at St. Ignatius High School, won the 2015 International Yo-Yo Championship. I can't tell you where competition was held, or who won this year, and I don't even know how to "walk the dog."

I actually wrote the first draft of this chapter before the 2016 NBA playoffs. When the Cavs pulled off their historic comeback, beating the Warriors, a.k.a. "the best team ever," I needed to write a do-over. The day prior to game seven, I was torn between wanting to side with my old friends, neighbors, and hometown to pull for the Cavs and rooting for the Warriors to preserve my already written chapter.

When the Cavaliers won, I'll admit, I did tear up just a little, but not as embarrassingly as LeBron James. Of course, he had something to cry about. According to many sports pundits, in one night he just went from a passive, error-prone, lacking in leadership, definitely not a Top Ten player to become "The Greatest Player of All Time." I sure wouldn't want to be in a relationship with a

Quicken Loans Arena is home to the Cleveland Cavaliers and a number of other professional sports teams

sports pundit. One minute you're the love of their life, and then an attractive waitress walks by or an old high school crush befriends them on Facebook.

Prior to June 19, 2016, the Cavaliers' success was merely from a Clevelander's starved-for-anything perspective. The team won the Eastern Conference in 2007 only to be swept by the Spurs. Then they were thoroughly beaten upside the head in the 2015 championship series with the Warriors. And the year after they won one, the Cavs were again outmanned by the Warriors, who'd picked up Kevin Durant. As I write, rumors are swirling that LeBron may become the double-dip-un-chosen-one if he leaves The Land for La-La-Land.

LeBron James, christened the Chosen One and the next Michael Jordan as a seventeen-year-old high school junior with a *Sports Illustrated* cover, went on to be Cleveland's most beloved athlete as the Cavs #1 pick in 2003. Later he became its most hated when he announced "The Decision" on live TV that he'd be taking his talents to South Beach. Fans burned his jerseys on the streets of Cleveland. But then the city took him back like a battered wife takes back her drunken, sleeveless–T-shirt–wearing husband when LeBron returned to Cleveland as the Re-Chosen One in 2014.

Long before LeBron, Cleveland fans got to Bear Witness to terrible basketball. They had only three winning seasons their first sixteen years. Cavs owner Ted Stepien remains the only owner in the history of the NBA who was *ordered* by the Commissioner to not make any more trades. His maneuvering was so awful that the team was becoming unwatchable.

The highlight of the first two decades was a playoff game where Craig Ehlo hit a shot to give the Cavs the lead over the Bulls with three seconds left—or just enough time for a young Michael Jordan to hit his first of many game-winning baskets.

Cleveland-lubbers probably feel I should gush more about the Cavs championship. Maybe I refuse to gush because the 2016

Cavs parade of 1.3 million beat out the 2010 New Orleans Saints parade of 800,000 as the largest per capita parade in sports history. Do I say "they beat us" or "we beat us?" Cleveland and New Orleans both agree that five million was a pathetic turnout for the Cubs parade in 2017. Chicago didn't even turn out the whole city.

★ ★ ★

As I discovered in my return trip, getting tickets to a pro sporting event in Cleveland is not impossible. I saw an Indians game at Progressive Field. Locally, it is often called The Jake in reference to the stadium's earlier name, Jacobs Field. That was before Progressive coughed up $58 million to rename the stadium. When it opened, the seating capacity was 42,865, and between 1995 and 2001 the team sold out 455 consecutive regular-season games. In a manner that may only make sense in Cleveland, the seating capacity was then reduced to 35,051. Maybe the owners feel the currently competitive team just can't last.

Progressive Field has been the home of the Cleveland Indians since 1994

The Browns play at FirstEnergy Stadium, a.k.a. The Factory of Sadness. It is one of only two NFL stadiums that have yet to host a postseason game.

Quicken Loans Arena was formerly Gund Arena. Here, locals call it The Q rather than hanging on to The Gund. The Cavs play here, along with the Cleveland Monsters (ice hockey) and the Cleveland Gladiators (arena football). The Gladiators were recently honored when Brent Overholt was named the AFL's Equipment Manager of the Year! The equipped football team, however, after going 17-1 in the 2014 season came up short (forty points short) in the championship. They haven't had a winning season since.

In a city that loves its sports teams and a city where watching a game outdoors can involve rain parkas or winter coats, sports bars flourish. To name the best sports bars in Cleveland is nearly as hard as naming all the sports bars. It's kind of a you-pick-'em prospect. With apologies to loyal customers of Rookies, Scalpers, and others, I'll note a few from a list of many.

Hooley House Sports Pub & Grille has three locations, but I'd head first to the one at 10310 Cascade Crossing location in Brooklyn, or closest to the heart of the city action. Hooley is an Irish term for "boisterous party," a noisy, merry, informal event, usually held in someone's home kitchen. Attendees brought their favorite dish, instruments, and favorite brew, and they ate, sang, and danced long into the night. Seems like an ideal setting to root for a Cavs win or find comfort among friends after a Browns loss.

Becky's (1762 East 18th St.) is a timeless hole in the wall with a delightful mix of sports fans, cab drivers, CSU students, and solitary hard-ass hard-stuff drinkers. A patron said, "These new places need to spend a lot of money on stuff to attract new people. Becky's has loyal people coming back because nothing has changed in forever."

Flannery's Pub (323 Prospect Ave.) is a quintessential Irish pub, located in the heart of it all, on the corner of East 4th Street and Prospect Avenue. It's a nightlife hotspot, a pub with a varied drink selection, Irish pub fare, and (the reason for mentioning it here) plenty of TV screens.

The Boneyard (5900 Mayfield Rd., Mayfield Heights) is maybe the largest sports bar you'll ever see. The space was an old movie theater, and they still use the old full-size theater screen to show Browns games. Genius! From the outside it looks like a Disney park theme castle or the world's largest indoor putt-putt course.

The Ice House Tavern & Grill (10036 Brookpark Rd., Brooklyn) is a big time Browns bar with a big time food like Macho Nachos. They are loaded with ground beef, jalapenos, lettuce, tomatoes, olives, and oozing liquid nacho cheese.

The Clevelander (834 Huron Rd.) was the one and only sports bar that made it on to more than one Best Of list. With numerous other bars and clubs within walking distance, The Clevelander is a best spot if you have plans for a night on the town after the game is over. Before and after Indians games, The Clevelander runs specials on food and drink.

Clark Bar (1201 Clark Ave.) is a vintage bar, believed (by some) to date back to an unverifiable 1880s. One patron claims he's been sitting on the same stool for decades. Clark has an excellent vibe and is filled with old timers reliving when the Browns were good.

Muldoon's (1020 E. 185th St.) is the best place to go if you like your sports viewing LOUD. They also have excellent fish fry.

Maple Grove (14832 Pease Rd.) is a working-class joint for regulars and locals looking for a laid-back reprieve from a lousy job, a broken home, or . . . the Browns.

Bob Golic's Sports Bar and Grille (1213 W. 6th St.) sort of has to make my list. Here you might take in a Browns game with the ex-Browns great. Maybe you can ask him that question about his brother.

CHAPTER FIVE

Let's Not Make a Scene

THE MUSIC OF CLEVELAND

I wanna be famous, I'm going to move to Cleveland.　　*—Stiv Bators*

*A*LMOST SINCE THEIR FOUNDING IN 1918, THE CLEVELAND Orchestra has been considered one of the best in the world. Any brochure (now website) pitching the virtues of Cleveland and why you should move there or relocate your business there will always mention two things: Metro Parks and the world-class orchestra. They rarely mention the weather.

Aside from the orchestra, Cleveland has never really been known as a musical hotbed. Detroit, from Motown to techno, seems more essential to music history. Nearby Akron might even overshadow Cleveland with their claim to Chrissie Hynde, the Black Keys, and DEVO. Even with the Rock & Roll Hall of Fame, Cleveland's actual legacy remains under the radar.

Yes, Alan Freed is the guy who said the words "rock and roll" on the radio in Cleveland, apparently changing the course of human history. And Cleveland's radio rock station, WMMS, is considered one of the most influential and greatest of all time.

WMMS, which really stood for Metro Media Stereo, was said

to stand for "Where Music Means Something" and later "Weed Makes Me Smile." *Rolling Stone* magazine chose WMMS as the best in the country for nine straight years (1979–87).

WMMS was known for their uncanny ability to spot new talent. They were one of the first radio stations to air live concerts, as they did for Lou Reed, Warren Zevon, and John Mellencamp. WMMS is largely credited as playing a key role in the breaking out of Rush, Roxy Music, Bruce Springsteen, Southside Johnny, Fleetwood Mac, Meat Loaf, the Pretenders, the New York Dolls, Lou Reed, Mott the Hoople, Boston, David Bowie, and Cheap Trick.

Key to their success was keeping on-air personalities fundamentally unchanged for many years. For radio aficionados, Kid Leo, Jeff and Flash, Matt the Cat, Id Stein, Denny Sanders, Murray Saul, Debbie Ullman, Betty "Crash" Korvan, Ruby Cheeks, BLF Bash, TR, and the late Len "Boom" Goldberg reads like the Murderer's Row of the old New York Yankees.

I listened (in minor horror) to WMMS during my return trip

A popular photo-op location at the Rock and Roll Hall of Fame

driving around the city. Fed by a continuous stream of Led Zeppelin, Stone Temple Pilots, Nirvana, and Smashing Pumpkins, I felt like WMMS was trying to recapture their crown as best radio station (1979–87). I asked "What happened?" and locals told me the radio station was bought out and WMMS kingpin John Gordon, who is himself in the Rock & Roll Hall of Fame, left to create oWOW in 2015.

Now, as far as what the Rock & Roll Hall of Fame is doing in Cleveland rather than Memphis, Chicago, New York, Detroit, or San Francisco, the Hall itself likes to say rock and roll was invented in Cleveland. That is only true if you focus exclusively on the phrase itself, "rock and roll," being coined by then–Cleveland DJ Alan Freed. Cleveland's actual rock scene was dominated by the infinitely forgettable Raspberries and Moonglow. The Raspberries biggest "hit" song, "Go All the Way," is probably best known for being background music in the 2014 Marvel superhero movie *Guardians of the Galaxy*.

Freed was on the air in Cleveland only from 1951 to '54, when he moved to New York. Freed did, during his brief tenure, organize what is kinda sorta considered the first rock 'n' roll concert. A five-act show called the Moondog Coronation Ball was set for March 21, 1952, at the Cleveland Arena. Huge crowds showed up in numbers far beyond the arena's seating, standing, or squeezing-in capacity. The Moondog was forced to shut down due to overcrowding and a near-riot. The failed concert actually added greatly to the popularity of rock 'n' roll. Now it seemed rebellious.

The Hall of Fame is open every day, 10 a.m. to 5:30 p.m. It ain't cheap: general admission is $23.50. But once inside, you'll find more than Michael Jackson's sequined glove (which IS there) and James Brown's jumpsuit with "SEX" spelled out in rhinestones (which IS there). You'll also find the unexpected cub scout uniform of Jim Morrison, Jimi Hendrix's childhood drawing of his father asleep on the couch, and Slash's pinball machine, which he claimed was the loudest pinball machine in history. The extensive Beatles collection spans from John Lennon's grade school report card to the drum kit used by Ringo Starr for their final concert.

It's kind of an insult to Cleveland that the induction ceremonies for the Cleveland-based museum have been held in Cleveland only four times while being held twice in Los Angeles and twenty-five times in New York City.

For many, the legacy of Cleveland bands begins and ends with the James Gang, formed in Cleveland in 1966. The band had a sniff of success with the singles "Funk #49" and "Walk Away." Frontman Joe Walsh walked away in 1975 to become a member of the Eagles. And you know what they say about the Eagles. ("I hate the fucking Eagles, man!" —Jeffrey "The Dude" Lebowski.) Ranker places the James Gang #433 among the best rock groups of all time, sandwiched in between the Tragically Hip and George Michael.

Raspberries were a power pop rock band formed in 1970. They were known for their clean-cut image, with short-hair and matching suits, which brought them teenybopper fandom and scorn from reviewers, who thought them decidedly uncool. Raspberries didn't even make the Ranker list. Their best known songs include "Go All the Way," "Let's Pretend," "I Wanna Be with You," "Tonight," and "Overnight Sensation." There are still passionate apologists who roll out more reasons than HRC supporters as to why the group didn't "win" more fame. Their lack of super-group status is most often blamed on not enough promotion and radio indifference. Said an executive at their label, Capitol Records, "We were so busy promoting acts like Grand Funk Railroad and Steve Miller that we lost focus on bands that mattered, like Raspberries."

★ ★ ★

In the 1970s there were flirtations with Cleveland becoming the white-hot center as punk capital of America. Stiv Bators was The Land's undeniable scrawny and snarling king. He was born in nearby Youngstown, but moved to Cleveland with a quote that should be as locally famous as Tennessee Williams's "America has only three cities: New York, San Francisco, and New Orleans. Everywhere else is Cleveland." Stiv said, "I wanna be famous, I'm going to move to Cleveland."

As the lead singer and driving force of the Dead Boys, Bators, as much as Joey Ramone or Sid Vicious, was the pioneer of the punk rock sound, look, and attitude. He was known for profanity, lewd gestures, and slashing his stomach with the mic stand. Guitarist Cheetah Chrome was likewise a punk star. When most punk performers jumped around and smashed things with a general disdain for musical talent, Cheetah was a revolutionary performer. He could actually play the hell out of the guitar.

The Dead Boys left Cleveland in 1976 to become the featured and beloved staple at New York's East Village fabled club, CBGB. Their debut album, *Young Loud and Snotty*, included the "hit" "Sonic Reducer," which is considered a punk rock classic and has been covered by Pearl Jam. When the Dead Boys flamed out in 1979, Stiv Bators became involved with a variety of bands, including Hormones, the Lords of the New Church, the Wanderers, and the Whores of Babylon (with Dee Dee Ramone and Johnny Thunders).

Bators was struck by a taxi in Paris. He was taken to a hospital but reportedly walked out after waiting several hours and before seeing a doctor. He died that night. There's a variety of stories about Stiv's next gig. One rumor is that his ashes were spread over Jim Morrison's grave at Père Lachaise Cemetery in Paris. Another is that his widow, Caroline, snorted his ashes to be closer to him. And a third, as claimed on Bebe Buell's Facebook page, is that his wife gave his ashes to Bebe. "Caroline gave me his ashes and told me he would want me to have them," she wrote. Bebe was Stiv's ex-girlfriend, former model, Playmate of the Month, and legendary groupie, having "been" with Todd Rundgren, Elvis Costello, Rod Stewart, Jimmy Page, Mick Jagger, and Steven Tyler, with whom she had their daughter, actress Liv Tyler.

Prior to the Dead Boys, members of the band had been the backbone of Rocket From the Tombs. Rocket From the Tombs is considered by some music writers and fans one of the greatest bands you've never heard, largely because they never recorded an album. You can find taped live recordings and demos circulated as bootlegs. A collection cobbled together after RFTT disbanded is titled *The Day the Earth Met the Rocket From the Tombs*. The front sleeve cover claims, "Live from Punk Ground Zero—Cleveland."

The backup and second most important punk band from the area was The Cramps. Their front man, Erick Lee Purkhiser, better known by his stage name Lux Interior, met his wife and band mate, Kristy Wallace, a.k.a. Poison Ivy, a.k.a. Ivy Rorschach, in Sacramento, when he picked her up hitchhiking.

Like so much Cleveland music, Ghoulardi was a huge influence on The Cramps. They titled their 1990 *Stay Sick* album in homage to him. When Ernie Anderson died, they dedicated their 1997 album, *Big Beat From Badsville*, to the memory of Ghoulardi.

The Cramps called their musical style psychobilly, originally claiming it to have been inspired by a Johnny Cash song, "One Piece at a Time," and later admitting any Cash reference was just to fuck with reviewers heads.

Lux Interior was known for his frenetic and provocative stage gyrations, with near-nudity as his skintight leather pants kept sliding down, and sexually suggestive movements. His signature move was the microphone blow job, where he could get the entire head of an SM-58 microphone into his mouth.

The Cramps, like the Dead Boys, left Cleveland for the dark corners and the graffiti-covered toilets of CBGB in New York. The band split after the death of Lux Interior in 2009.

Foreign Bodies, Jim Jones, Dave E. and the Cool Marriage Counselors, Golden Palominos, the Wild Giraffes, and the Styrenes were all proto-punk bands that stayed in the area.

John D. Morton formed the Electric Eels with guitarist Brian McMahon and singer Dave E. McManus. "We thought we were going to be extremely popular," Morton says. "Dave and I really worked on it immensely and with strident purpose. We were really taken aback when we weren't."

Morton and the Eels were inspired by three sources. The Velvet Underground played at Le Cave on Euclid Avenue and blew them away. Like all Clevelanders at the time, Ghoulardi was a huge influence. And lastly, they attended a Captain Beefheart concert, thought the band totally sucked, and were inspired by a "we can do better than that" rallying cry.

The Eels were said to represent "something new, a cultivation of the potential for physical violence." Morton, in particular, would go out of his way to provoke audiences. Playing a blue-collar bar, Brian MacMahon recalls, "We weren't a homosexual couple, just two males dancing with each other in order to mind-fuck the drunken lumpen prole patrons."

The band started out playing in Columbus, Ohio, because John D. thought his life might be in danger due to a jealous husband back in Cleveland. I guess in his mind, jealous husbands weren't able to drive south two hours on I-71.

After the Eels disbanded in 1975, John formed his next group, X—X, and their not-quite-hit song, "You're Full of Shit." He created the lesser-known Johnny and the Dicks with their set ending anthem, "Cleveland Sucks."

The CLEPunk website currently lists nearly 150 more punk bands in Cleveland, including Baloney Heads, the Babushka Men, Kneecappers, Lepers, Ringworm, and McShitz. Yeah, I've never heard of any of them either.

Considered by many critics and fans as Cleveland's best ever band, Pere Ubu regard themselves as more "avant-garage" (mixing avant garde and garage band) than punk. They were called "thrillingly unorthodox and cerebral rock music" by *The Guardian*. Over the course of sixteen albums spread over thirty-five-plus years, the only constant has been lead singer Dave Thomas. Other members have left the band or died.

Thomas may be the least typical front man, combining the spastic moves of Joe Cocker with the unkempt looks of Zero Mostel. He's been described as possessing a "disturbing whale-like fat warble of a singing voice."

Then there are the Easter Monkeys, a band not so much forgotten as barely noticed. Called "menacing rock 'n' roll," they never got airplay on Cleveland's premier radio station, WMMS. When they played at the legendary Agora, they were shoved in the creepy basement rather than the main stage where Bruce Springsteen played along with Talking Heads, Kiss, Judas Priest, Metallica, U2, the Clash—pretty much every band of importance.

Singer Chris Yarmock said, "People mistakenly saw us as a punk band. But we were a psychedelic jazz band that loved all kinds of music and everything Ghoulardi." Jim Lanza, who hosted a local radio show in the '80s, claimed the Easter Monkeys "were so powerful that I felt hypnotized when I saw them.

I'd never seen anything like them before—and I haven't seen anything like them since."

Bridging the gap between Cleveland's music history and current scene would be 15 60 75. The group's name was derived from multiplying increments of 15 based on 1, 4 and 5—in a musician's world, the universal progression. Fans were utterly confused and simply called them the Numbers Band.

Since their start at Kent State in the '70s, with their first performance two weeks after the famous "four dead in Ohio" campus shootings, there have been three constants: Bob Kidney, Jack Kidney, and Terry Hynde (older brother of Chrissie Hynde). Over the last nearly fifty years (and counting), their music has never been in step. The band has been called both "outdated" and "ahead of its time." With the rise of New Age and Punk, they were called "the old guys on the street who play the blues." Their style actually straddles blues, jazz, and rock.

While loved by critics and music publications—*Rolling Stone* calling them "this country's greatest under-known cult band"—the Numbers Band never achieved fame. Bob Kidney explained, "We are not interested in making hits, we are interested in making history."

They play often at Beachland Ballroom and Nighttown in Cleveland, as well as weekly sets at the Venice Cafe in Kent.

Chris Butler was a member of the Numbers Band, but was dumped when he blew off a rehearsal. I first met Chris when he joined his then partner, Maria Reidelbach, as she came to New Orleans to help me create a putt-putt course (that never got built). That first trip, I learned three essential things about Chris: 1) He was the creator of the hit pop song "I Know What Boys Like," 2) he graduated from the same high school as me, and 3) he currently lives in the house just south of Cleveland where mass murderer Jeffrey Dahmer grew up and made his first kill.

Since then, I have learned Chris has a rich personal history (he was among the crowd of students at Kent State fired on by the Ohio National Guard, which left four dead), and even richer and more varied musical and creative endeavors.

He started his professional musical career playing guitar in a blues band, City Lights, then followed fellow musician Jack Kidney to form the Numbers Band. He still claims Bob Kidney as his overwhelming mentor and #1 influence in music, with a smaller nod to Ghoulardi for attitude. After they cut him loose, Chris joined Tin Huey. They signed a recording contract but never found a wide audience. Tin Huey band members continue to drift apart and regroup in various new configurations (Half Cleveland, Ralph's Carnage, Harvey in the Hall).

Butler hit the little big time with his group The Waitresses, for whom he wrote the residuals-rich songs "Christmas Wrapping," used as the theme song for the TV show *Square Pegs*, and his signature hit, "I Know What Boys Like." The latter song has been used in episodes of *The Simpsons, Family Guy, Nip/Tuck,* and *Californication*, plus the movies *I Was a Teenage Zombie, Another Gay Movie,* and *The Last American Virgin*. Covers of "I Know What Boys Like" have been recorded by Vitamin C, the girl band Shampoo, Katharine McPhee, and Tracey Ullman.

For his more recent forays, Chris has been called "that little engine of art and commerce." He has more creative projects under way at any given time than a hound dog does fleas.

He was a writer for and co-editor of *Music, Computers and Software* magazine. He produced Freedy Johnston's album *The Trouble Tree*. He formed another band, purple k'niF (one of Ghoulardi's signature phrases). They were a "Maximum Surf 'n' Twang" instrumental/surf/hot rod/juvenile delinquent band that's still playing into their third decade. He undertook a four-year gig as a drummer and bandleader for a stage band on the Comedy Central TV show *Two Drink Minimum*. He founded Future Fossil Records, and released his first full-length album, *I Feel A Bit Normal Today*.

I asked him what he's working on right now. "I'm working on my second short film, sort of a faux TED Talk about a ridiculous lamp from the '50s which has evolved to become a major artifact from the mid-twentieth century. Since I did pretty well with a holiday song, I'm writing a few more songs inspired by obscure holidays, partnering with Tin Huey reed man Ralph Carney. . . . I'm also playing in Half Cleveland with Harvey Gold (from Tin Huey), our vehicle for our new songs and cool covers.

I am rehearsing with some folks to recreate a radio play version of *Sunset Boulevard* for a theater festival in early June. I play the William Holden role, where I'm dead at the beginning of the story . . . then it's all downhill from there."

If you see a pattern in all his creative endeavors, please let me know.

Chris also holds the Guinness World Record for the longest pop song recording in history, a sixty-nine-minute song entitled "The Devil Glitch." The project has now been expanded online as "The Infinite Glitch," which is accepting additions to the song in the hopes that eventually it will play for days. Currently at 4:41:44, Chris still considers it too short.

In my utterly unjustifiable opinion, the most Cleveland of the current Cleveland bands is Archie and the Bunkers. There's very much a Ghoulardi vibe going on even though the two brothers, Emmett and Cullen O'Connor, were born some forty years after Ghoulardi left the airwaves. The video for their song "Knifuli Knifula" actually uses old-time Ghoulardi clips.

Matt Fields, a booker and manager at the Beachland Ballroom, said, "These guys are frickin' stars, man. The first time I saw them my jaw hit the floor. Every time they play, within two songs everybody at the bar has left their seats to go stand in front of the stage to watch and listen to them. I haven't felt this strongly about a new band in a long time."

My muddled handle would position Archie and the Bunkers as if Jim Morrison sat in as the singer with the B-52s. They've been self-described as "Hi-Fi Organ Punk" and by others as follows: "On stage, the siblings attack their songs with an energy that whips the audience into a frenzy. The unique growl of Cullen's whirring, overdriven organ and the driving beat of Emmett's 4-piece drum kit, leave concert-goers in shock at the sonic assault levied by only two."

For many others, Welshly Arms is the most Cleveland of Cleveland bands. They are self-described as a mixture of blues, rhythm and soul, and rock that creates a "fresh throwback sound that represents Midwestern roots." Their root influences are Jimi Hendrix (Seattle), Otis Redding (Georgia), Howlin' Wolf (Mississippi), and the Temptations (OK, finally we've got in a Midwestern Detroit). Quentin Tarantino, in his film *The Hateful Eight*, mixed their cover of Sam and Dave's "Hold On, I'm Coming" with Ennio Morricone's soundtrack.

That song now joins my personal list of best cover songs of all time, joining Jimi Hendrix doing such a great cover of "All Along the Watchtower" that most people think it's his original song.

John Petkovic, in addition to being the front man in many bands, including Cobra Verde, Death of Somalia, and Sweet Apple (where he's been called "provocative grime" by *Rolling Stone*), is best known in Cleveland as the longtime arts and entertainment writer for *The Plain Dealer*.

Petkovic's pièce de résistance is the Tragical History Tour, which he penned in 2015. It is a sight-seeing trip with absolutely no sights to see. His tour takes you to historic spots that no longer exist where rock 'n' roll thrived. Along the journey, you'll visit 3717 Euclid Avenue, where the Cleveland Arena used to be and hosted, or tried to host, the first ever rock concert, the Moondog Coronation Ball.

At 7500 Euclid Avenue you'll see a grocery store standing on the spot once occupied by Leo's Casino, a seven-hundred-person capacity club where Smokey Robison, the Supremes, John Coltrane, Ray Charles, the Temptations, and Otis Redding all once played.

La Cave, at 10615 Euclid Avenue, hosted the Velvet Underground, Neil Young, and Jeff Beck. Closed in 1969, it is now a parking lot.

Swingos, on East 18th Street and Euclid Avenue, from 1971 to '82 welcomed Led Zeppelin, Cher, Gene Simmons, and Elvis. It is now a sapless Comfort Inn Motel.

Wesley Brite & the Honeytones are from Akron, but most of their live gigs will be in Cleveland clubs like Beachland Ballroom, House of Blues, the ECU, and Cleveland festivals Brite Winter Fest, Larchemere Porchfest, and Cleveland Flea Holiday Market Party. The sound is pure soul and funk. Wesley's showstopping performances have been compared to greats like Al Green and Otis Redding. Introduced to live audiences as "the Sultan of Soul," I would dare compare him to the Godfather of Soul himself. His backing band isn't up there with Macao Parker, Fred Wesley, and Pee Wee Ellis—i.e., the greatest horn section in history—but they give it an admirable shot. The Honeytones mimic the dance steps of James Brown's band. Wesley peppers his songs with James Brown–like signature grunts and yelps.

Mushroomhead is straight-ahead, head-banging industrial metal. The scary mask-wearing band has been around since 1993. The group reached a high point in 2014 when their eighth studio album, *The Righteous and The Butterfly*, debuted at Number Twenty on the Billboard chart.

They're not for everyone's taste, including Mushroomhead's former lead singer, Waylon Reavis. After twelve years with the band, Waylon baled, stating, "They're not good people . . . I hope they die slowly. I wish I had never met 'em."

Reavis has formed his own new band, A Killer's Confession, that he promises will "knock your dick in the dirt." I assume he intends delivering on that promise to be a good thing.

There's a number of lo-fi, lyrics-driven performers whose talent seems inspired by or a perfect accompaniment to Cleveland's endless days without sunshine.

Extra Medium Pony's album title, *Meaninglessness*, says it all. Singer songwriter Rick Spitalsky seems to take pleasure in gloom. Another album is named *11868* and refers to 11868 Clifton Boulevard in Lakewood. It's where he met and was painfully dumped by his ex-girlfriend. Spitalsky has said, "depression is a lifelong battle, not a wet fart. You can quote me on that." You've heard athletes or musicians say they could practically perform in their sleep. Bring up the video for Extra Medium Pony's song "Get It Together" and you'll see what performing in one's sleep actually looks like.

Max Sollisch, a.k.a. Dolfish, has been a workmanlike songsmith, deeply rooted in Cleveland with songs like "Collinwood" and "Euclid Beach." I admire his lyric writing à la Neil Young or Bruce Springsteen, but then he willfully stumbles off the expected track and dips into a vibe a bit like Antsy Pants or Moldy Peaches.

But let's acknowledge the elephant in the room. His singing voice sounds most like SpongeBob SquarePants. Defenders say his weird voice perfectly fits the material like the nontraditional singing of Bob Dylan or Tom Waits.

That's all to say nothing of other musicians, like Marcus Alan Ward, described as "Prince arm wrestling Frank Ocean after gobbling a handful of shrooms at a Moody Blues pool party, while D'Angelo spins the classics;" Case Bargè, who's dealt with real issues like homelessness, being robbed at gun point, having a hernia in his brain, learning to walk again, and not just over-cast skies; Fresh Produce, a great female hip-hop duo; Cities & Coasts; The Lighthouse and the Whaler; Maura Rogers & The Bellows; Heavenly Queen; Midnight Passenger; and All Dino-saurs, whom tab themselves, "We feel more like a punk band. But we want to play faster and be heavier. We wanted to see what we could accomplish without actually being good at our instruments." I simply can't get to all of Cleveland's music in a mere chapter.

However, just as you can't wrap up Cleveland's food culture with-out a nod to their butchers, you aren't done with Cleveland's music until you mention polka.

Polka swept America in the 1840s. Cleveland was called "America's Polka Capital," and early classics like "The Put-in-Bay Polka" (1871) and "The Irresistible Schottische" (1885) were cre-ated by area bands. There were Polka radio shows on Cleveland stations WGAR, WHK, WJAY, and WTAM. Two polka monthlies were published, *Polka News & Events* and *Polkarama*, plus a news-paper, *Polka Scene*.

Cleveland is today home to the national Polka Hall of Fame. Clevelander Frankie Yankovic, no relation to Weird Al, is consid-ered the Polka King.

Frankie Yankovic was born to Slovene immigrant parents and

raised in Collinwood after his family bolted from West Virginia, a step ahead of the law. They'd been bootleggers.

Frankie released over two hundred records in his career, sold thirty million copies, and somehow managed to perform more than three hundred live shows a year. He also drove six hours to and from Buffalo each week to host the radio show *Polka Time*. In 1986 he was awarded the first-ever Grammy given to a polka recording. The Grammys took a disappointing course when they eliminated polka as a category in 2009.

On the day before Pearl Harbor, Frankie opened a tavern called the Yankovic Bar. The bar became the hangout for top polka musicians. It was sort of the CBGB or Apollo Theater for the passionately unhip.

Yankovic's song "Who Stole the Kishka?" is a Cleveland classic. It used to be performed every Friday night on Ghoulardi's TV show whenever anyone said (by design or by accident) "Parma." Parma is Cleveland's primary Polish community. Frankie's other "hits" include "In Heaven There Is No Beer" and the rather non-P.C., "I Don't Want Her. You Can Have Her She's Too Fat for Me."

Other classic polka bands in The Land include the Cleveland Society of Danube Swabians' Brass Band & Posaunenchor—or DSB&P for kinda short, now nearing sixty years of oompah—and the DMV, not the Department of Motor Vehicles but Deutscher Music Verein, or German Music Society, and Frank Moravcik and his Magic Buttons.

There is my personal favorite, the Chardon Polka Band. They look different than every other polka band. If you took away their accordion and matching bowling-style shirts, you could easily think you're looking at a Seattle grunge band. In 2003, frontman Jake Kouwe, as a high school kid, pulled together the band in the school's music room. They started out playing at local senior centers and nursing homes in the Chardon area. They now tour nationwide from New Jersey to New Mexico.

They sound different. Band members come from all manner of

musical backgrounds. Joe Dahlhausen is a former heavy metal drummer, sax player Emily Burke comes from a background in classical music. While the group plays traditional polkas, they break out their own written tunes along with polka-pop covers of "Wipe Out" by the Ventures and Twisted Sisters' "We're Not Going to Take It." They even have drum solos, which ain't your tata's Polka.

They think different. Jake has said, "Everybody and their brother gets a guitar and starts a garage band. Everybody and their brother doesn't start a polka band anymore. I would like polka to be the next punk rock." Their website is entitled "Polka with Attitude!"

As to where to experience live polka while you're in town, Sachsenheim Hall (7001 Denison Ave.) opened as a social hall for Germans in 1910 and has since evolved into a ballroom, dance hall, solarium, and biergarten all rolled into one. Current manager Scott "Grumpy" Lindell has turned the club into a multi-ethnic spot. There's still live polka and Friday night dances. But you can also go there for Taco Tuesdays.

Sterle's Country House (1401 E 55th St.) has been in business for fifty years, with Margot Clinski running the joint for the last twenty-two. On Friday nights, you can dine and dance from 6 p.m. to 9 p.m. Saturday night it's 8 p.m. to midnight.

Beachland Ballroom is more known as a rock venue. But during the biting January days, always a slow month for Cleveland clubs, owner Cindy Barber had the whim to try out Polka Brunch. Hugely successful, Polka Brunch is now every Sunday, 11 a.m. to 3 p.m.

The Happy Dog Saloon (5801 Detroit Ave.) started hosting Polka Happy Hour one Friday a month. DJ Kishka, a.k.a. Justin Gorski, wears lederhosen, a fake beard, and a little green alpine hat with a feather.

Wednesday nights at Karlin Hall (5304 Fleet Ave.) is Polka Night. It was founded in 1935 by three lodges of the Czech Fraternal Insurance Society of the Catholic Workmen.

Hofbräuhaus (1550 Chester Ave.) is actually a chain, with locations in Columbus and Cincinnati, Ohio, as well as Chicago, Pittsburgh, Las Vegas, and St. Petersburg, Florida. However, in the polka capital, there are twelve to fifteen live sessions each and every week. Performing in the Cleveland location have been Cleveland's own the Brian Papesh Band, Anthony Culkar, Bob Kravos, the Casuals, the Chardon Polka Band, the Cleveland Society of Danube Swabians' Brass Band & Posaunenchor, Der Muzik Box, Deutscher Musik Verein, Ed Klimczak, Eric Noltkamper, Fred Ziwich and his International Sound Machine, Gottscheer Blaskapelle, Joey Tomsick and the Shotskis, Kordupel-Culkar Band, Mike Wojtila, Patty C and the Guys, Polka Revolution, PROSIT-teers!, and Schnickelfritz, which has become the de facto late-night house band at Hofbräuhaus.

I doubt there's another city in America where a club could pull from twenty local polka bands.

CHAPTER SIX

Bars, Clubs & Bowling

NIGHTLIFE IN CLEVELAND

I think this is the best situation for me, 'cause there's nothing but basketball. There's nothing. There's no going out. There's no late nights. There's video games, basketball, and basketball.

—*J.R. Smith, on being traded to the Cleveland Cavaliers*

*A*S REVEALED ELSEWHERE IN THIS BOOK, NIGHTLIFE IN CLEVE-land during my years there was watching Ghoulardi after the 11 p.m. news and blowing up mailboxes. On occasion we would also replace the foam in fire extinguishers with pressurized water and do drive-by drenchings of bikers and pedestrians. Again, we were "the good kids."

In high school, a group of friends would also occasionally pile into the back of Lou Carlisle's van (Lou's nickname was "Sewer Mouth") and sneak into the old Roxy Burlesque Theater for some adult entertainment. I swear I never once joined them.

The Roxy closed in 1977 after forty-five years of titillating lewdness. They were located in an area called "Short Vincent," for Vincent Avenue, a street only a single block in length. In its heyday, Short Vincent was the hub of Cleveland's nightlife. The Theatrical Grill, next to the Roxy, was run by the notorious owner Morris "Mushy" Wexler, and was a hangout where movie stars like Dean Martin and Julie Garland, passing through town, would rub elbows with local mobsters like Shondor Birns.

Roxy Burlesque saw top international performers like Blaze Starr, Tempest Storm, and Irma the Body grace their stage, with nationally known comedians like Abbott and Costello, Red Buttons, and Phil Silver performing in between acts. Most noteworthy was Carrie Finnell. Carrie set the record for longest striptease in history as she removed more and more slips of clothing, one item per week, during her fifty-four-week run on the Roxy stage. She is also credited for creating the art of tassel twirling. What she called her "educated bosom" could twirl in opposite directions or have one tassel spinning wildly while the other remained perfectly still.

The Beatles became Municipal Stadium's first ever concert in 1966. Nice inauguration. From 1974 to 1980, the World Series of Rock concerts were held there each summer, featuring acts such as the Rolling Stones, Pink Floyd, the Beach Boys, and Aerosmith. The Rolling Stones 1978 concert, with 82,238 attendees, was reportedly the first concert anywhere to gross over $1 million.

In the 1980s and 1990s, the stadium hosted concerts by the Jackson Five, Bruce Springsteen, U2, and the Who, with return visits by Pink Floyd and the Rolling Stones. The opening of the Rock & Roll Hall of Fame was celebrated with an all-star concert at the stadium which featured Chuck Berry, Bob Dylan, Aretha Franklin, and Jerry Lee Lewis.

Then, they tore down the stadium.

The Public Auditorium thereafter inherited the mantle as Cleveland's biggest venue. The Beatles and the Rolling Stones also played at the Auditorium, as did Elvis Presley, Jimi Hendrix, the Grateful Dead, Janis Joplin, and the Beastie Boys. In my teens, I saw three concerts there: Three Dog Night, Jefferson Starship, and Jethro Tull.

Today, the big venues are the Quicken Loans Arena, where the Cavs play, and the Bert L. and Iris S. Wolstein Center, often

The Cleveland Public Auditorium is a center for arts and culture called "The Convo," which is the indoor arena of Cleveland State University.

As a visitor to The Land, however, I'm guessing you're looking more for local musicians in more intimate clubs.

The Grog Shop (2785 Euclid Heights Blvd.) is a landmark near the once hippest area of Cleveland—Coventry. It was sort of our Haight Ashbury or New York's Greenwich Village. The bar and club opened right on Coventry Road but moved around the corner for more space in 2003. The Grog has maintained the intimacy and raw character for which it was known. They showcase live music 7 days a week, 365 days a year.

Numerous local and national touring bands stop by the Grog Shop, which has hosted bands like Supergrass, Dinosaur Jr., the Flaming Lips, Eek a Mouse, the Dandy Warhols, The Black Keys, and Oasis. While I revisited Cleveland, Drive-By Truckers performed there.

The Beachland Ballroom & Tavern (15711 Waterloo Rd.) started out in 1950 as the Croatian Liberty Home, with the ballroom and tavern. The Liberty Home was a top spot for social events and political rallies. It was a Cleveland landmark. Then, in 2000, it became Cleveland's most eclectic music club.

You can credit owner Cindy Barber as either a visionary or someone who made due with the best she could afford at the time. "I was looking to open a concert club and wanted to do a destination location in my neighborhood," Barber recalls. "There was some crime starting to happen, and I thought this might scare off some of the prostitutes and drugs. I also knew I couldn't afford to open a place in the Flats or downtown. Then I started looking at this old Croatian hall that had been on the market for three years." She ignored the cigarette-stained walls and brought in a sound man who confirmed, "Yes, this could be a good club."

Barber then approached Mark Leddy, who was booking garage and punk acts in the Flats, to be her partner. Opening night, March 2, 2000, was a punk band, the Tellers. The early years, they also attracted bands like the White Stripes in 2000 and The Black Keys in 2002, who would go on to fame but on those nights played to smaller crowds. It was actually The Black Keys' first live performance.

Beachland has become The Spot. Their name comes from the longtime nickname of the North Collinwood neighborhood. From 1894 until 1969, Euclid Beach Amusement Park operated nearby.

Today, Beachland routinely fills their intimate tavern (capacity 148) and a larger ballroom (capacity 500). They have now showcased more than twenty thousand bands, including The Cramps, Dave Davies, Los Lobos, Ricky Lee Jones, and Guided by Voices.

I didn't know the groups who played the Beachland during my visit (the Speedbumps, Strange Americans, Mt. Joy, Lydia Lunch Retrovirus, Old Salt Union, Sparrowmilk), but assuming you're cooler than me, you probably do. I was tempted by their Friday and Saturday night DEVOtional, a tribute to DEVO with cover bands.

The Winchester Tavern and Music Hall (12112 Madison Ave.) was, wasn't, and now is again one of Cleveland's coolest venues. Located in the area of Lakewood called Birdtown because of street names (Robin, Lark, Plover, and Thrush, among others), Winchester Music Hall attracted national touring acts and was a staple of the local music scene. From 2002 until they closed in 2014, it was called by Metromix "one of the hippest, and definitely most comfortable, old school music halls" in the city.

Shane Motolik, a native of Wakeman, Ohio, used to frequent the Winchester when he and friends would make the trip to Cleveland for open-mic nights. By the time he returned to Cleveland from Los Angeles in 2015, the Bevy in Birdtown had taken over the spot. When they closed, he jumped at the opportunity to reopen his favorite club. The Winchester was brought back to life on Memorial Day, 2017. "We're looking at monthly niche parties, electronic and dance nights, comedy, possibly even burlesque," says Motolik. "It's an incredible space and there's a lot of talented people in Cleveland."

Nighttown (12387 Cedar Rd.) touts itself as having the "ambiance of Irish pubs and turn of the century New York bars." It was named after the Dublin red-light district in James Joyce's *Ulysses*.

Along with other live music, it has some of the best jazz in Cleveland. Nighttown received national attention when it became the only club in Ohio to be featured on *DownBeat*'s list of the best jazz clubs in the world. In addition to booked acts, numerous musicians—from Wynton Marsalis to Stevie Wonder—have dropped in for impromptu performances.

As stellar as the drinks and the music, Nighttown has fabulous and historic artwork on the walls. Two paintings, named *Vote for Schmoe* and *Fifi LaSalle*, have been donated from the Press Club headquarters. The paintings are bettered by a huge mural painted by Bill Roberts that formerly hung at Kornman's, a restaurant on Short Vincent during its heyday of molls and mobsters.

Parkview Nite Club (1261 W. 58th St.) is the kind of place you head to after work to down a few beers. The place looks and smells like its eighty years of history. It is among the best places to hear the blues in Cleveland. There's a blues jam every Wednesday night.

Cleveland's House of Blues (308 Euclid Ave.) opened in 2004. The large club spans over sixty thousand square feet. Underneath the stage is a metal box of mud from the Mississippi Delta. I guess it adds a little Southern soul to performers who play there. As I came back to Cleveland, Rob Zombie was there one night and the Aquabats were there another, the latter a ska and synth band wearing matching superhero outfits.

Happy Dog (11625 Euclid Ave.—a.k.a. the Euc—and 5801 Detroit Ave.) were previously mentioned as food stops. They are as well known for their live music. The Euclid Tavern was one of Cleveland's legendary live music venues. Established in 1909, the "Euc" became a fixture on the local music scene in the 1970s and early 1980s under the ownership of Bob Jost and Paul Devito. Back then, regulars included Mr. Stress, the Numbers Band, Chrissie Hynde, and Peter Laughner. The bar served as the location for Paul Schrader's film *Light of Day*, starring Joan Jett and Michael J. Fox as members of a fictional band, the Barbreakers.

Sean Kilbane and Sean Watterson bought the Westside location in 2008 with the hopes of turning it into a go-to place to hear local music. Kilbane was tragically killed in an accident on the premises, but not before turning the club into a success once again.

The variety of music is nearly as expansive as the hot dog toppings. They present rock, country, punk, and polka. Sean Watterson thought he would try something different by inviting members of the Cleveland Orchestra to perform on stage. That night's success led to all sorts of collaborations including monthly talks by scientists, writers, and academics. John Petkovic noted in *The Plain Dealer*, "New Yorkers blow millions trying to make a new place look this authentic."

The Brothers Lounge (11607 Detroit Ave.) is a vintage establishment offering three bars that offer something for everyone. They have an intimate room with a piano man and larger spaces for every variety of music—the Bad Boys of Blues, Skatch Anderssen Orchestra (Big Band Jazz), All-In Country Band, a tribute night to John Lennon, and regular sessions with Chris Hatton's Musical

Circus. His circus is solo gigs where he plays a guitar, synthesizer, percussion, and a loop pedal.

Music Box Supper Club (1148 Main Ave.) has a downstairs supper club and an upstairs concert hall. They too offer a musical variety, including blues, jazz, soul, Americana, rock, punk, roots, and country. Headliners have included Lisa Loeb, 10,000 Maniacs, Big Bad Voodoo Daddy, Ginger Baker, Indigo Girls, John Hiatt, Concrete Blonde, Leon Russell, the English Beat, and the Smithereens. If there's not at least one in there that peaks your interest, I'd say music is not your thing.

For straight-up bars, Clevelanders also seem to love **Edison's Pub** (2373 Professor Ave.) and the **Velvet Tango Room** (2095 Columbus Rd.), but the former is (to me) pretty much standard fare—pizza, beer, and booths—and the latter scared me off with the "About Us" page alone ("Our owner is a man of mystery. After escaping from an unnamed country in Eastern Europe, he travelled to South America. Gradually, he made a name for himself in the tango bars of Buenos Aires, but when a price was put on his head by a jealous husband, he stowed away in the hold of a freighter he believed was headed to Marseilles . . ."). Is there a word for forced or fake irony?

West 25th is the hub of drinking spots. Great Lakes Brewing Co., Market Garden Brewery, Bier Markt, Bar Cento, ABC the Tavern, Town Hall, and Old Angle Tavern are all located within a just a few steps of one another. In my snotty opinion, the busy stretch feels like an area I might have enjoyed back in my twenties or after a fifth or sixth drink.

If dive bars are more "your thing," Cleveland has a dive bar called **Dive Bar** (1214 W. 6th St.). It is considered a people-watching mecca, with diverse jukebox selections from Backstreet Boys to Kanye West to Tom Petty.

WILL HOLLINGSWORTH

The star bartender currently mixing and pouring in The Land is proba-bly Will Hollingsworth. Born in California, raised in Oregon, educated in New Mexico, and employed in Washington, DC, before moving to Cleveland in 2009, Hollingsworth may seem like an off-kilter choice for essential Cleveland bartender. But in spirit, he is pure Cleveland, and I don't mean he wears a matching white belt and shoes.

Will came to Cleveland at age twenty-three, having just finished working for the 2008 Obama campaign and layered with advanced degrees in philosophy and history of math and science, with concen-trations in classics and comparative literature. He's like the opposite of Moe the bartender on *The Simpsons*.

"I was working in Washington, D.C., and hated it, and I took this road trip and stopped in Cleveland," he recalls. "I fell in love with the place and what it represented." For Hollingsworth, Cleveland rep-resents the idea "that America can be revived in these old places like Cleveland or Pittsburgh or Detroit or Buffalo. You know, places with history, that are real."

He came to the city with zero experience as a bartender. He would sit, night after night, at the Greenhouse Tavern with no solid plan and maxed-out credit cards. "Eventually I wore them down, and they hired me."

Will would move on to become the bartender at Michael Symon's Lolita, the whole time becoming obsessed with creating his own bar with his notion of the perfect bar atmosphere. He describes his vision as follows: "The perfect bar is the place where you start your night and end your night. It's the first place you go and it's the place you go when you've got a bottle of wine in you and you're looking a little disheveled and you want to be with your friends, sit in the dark, have a conversation and have fun."

The setting for his perfect bar presented itself when the old Union Gospel Press building was refurbished. The Union Gospel Press once housed a press for bibles and other religious materials, plus a monastery with the still-in-use stained-glass windows. The 160-year history of the place sparked the academic in Hollingsworth, but the timeworn walls and floor completely seduced him. "Look at this old and beautiful space—look at those walls, look how it's messy there on the brick." He points to his refurbished floor. "See this wood? This came from the floor of a barn located in central Ohio. Look, see how it's rough and worn. The doors of the barn were often left open all day, and this is a result of the sun beating down on this wood. You can't create something like this."

He feels the same passion for the drinks he serves. "I like to focus on simple drinks and do them well." He affirms, "A good thing is better by making it simpler rather than making it more complicated. All of the best drinks aren't terribly overwrought in their conception or execution." A man after my anti-foodie, piss-on-craft-cocktail heart, he's said, "I think the worst thing that ever happened to bartending is mixology. I feel that idea has nearly sounded the death of bartending. Give me a bottle of Jim Beam and a case of Miller Light."

"I am of the opinion that my generation wants the same thing out of a bar that our parents did: a place where you can meet people, feel comfortable, develop a relationship with your bartender. It's just a place where you go when you don't want to go home."

The bar that would most draw me in as a regular—if I lived in Cleveland (which I don't) and was a drinker (which I'm not)—would be **Hotz Cafe** (2529 W. 10th St.). They've been around since 1919, founded by a family of Russian immigrants. During Prohibition, visiting ballplayers Babe Ruth and Lou Gehrig are said to have called Hotz their favorite speakeasy. It's also said that when Grandpa Andy Hotz caught wind of Eliot Ness being in the area, he dumped all his illegal liquor in a neighbor's flowerbed.

Shelia Hotz currently runs the bar and begins each shift blowing kisses to the portraits hanging over the bar of John and Andy Hotz, her father-in-law and grandfather. She says, "I like to let them know I'm doing the best I can. In their time, they'd have a heart attack if they knew a woman was running the place."

ABC Tavern (1872 W. 25th St.) has been called "a punk-rock dive bar and true old-man dive bar way before the area got gentrified." The new owners were smart enough to keep the bar pretty much as it was (bowling machine and all). It has good food, a jukebox loaded with stoner rock and death metal, and cheap drinks.

One of the oldest bars in Cleveland is **Harbor Inn** (1219 Main Ave.). Back in 1895 it was a hangout for dock and factory workers. Now owned by Ken Kamila, who bought it in 2015 and added a first-time-ever draft-beer system, it was run for many years by Vlado "Wally" Pisorn, called the King of Slovenia.

One thing Kamila did not change is the practice of loudly ringing out last call using the 1895 Zenith City ship bell that hangs in the dead center of the bar. "We get a lot of neighbor complaints," Kamola says with a grin, "but we still do it anyway."

The Social Room (2261 Lee Rd.) is a traditional dive spot. They have cheap beer, a pool table, and darts. Most of the people slumped over the bar have been coming there for twenty years and used to know one another's names.

Benny owns **B and G Tavern** (4150 Lorain Ave.) but lets his son, VC, and daughter-in-law, Cynthia, run the joint. It's dimly lit, more out-of-date than nostalgic with old Spud Mackenzie signs. Chef Brett Sawyer considers their burgers the best in The Land. Almost every drink, beer, shot, or simple mixed drink is $2.

If the name **Ugly Broad Tavern** (3908 Denison Ave.) offends you, for god's sake please don't look at their logo. Their catchphrase, "The Best in Beer and Bullshit" is only slightly better. Rather than live music, the Ugly Broad has a life-sized cut out of John Wayne.

OK, you might be seeing a pattern by now. I wasn't done presenting Cleveland's food until I wrote about their butchers. I wasn't done with the music scene until I included polka. Writing about Cleveland's nightlife, I have to close with bowling.

Not mentioned in my sports chapter, Cleveland has more Hall of Fame bowlers than any other city. Joe Bodis, who won the 1924 championship bowling in street shoes, as well as "Skang" Mercurio in the '30s, John Klares, Walter Ward, J. Elmer Reed, and Harry Smith are among the all-time elite, even though I'm guessing you've never heard of any of them.

There are over twelve thousand bowling alleys in the United States. Of these twelve thousand, only twelve still use manual pin setters to reset their lanes. The ageless **Maple Lanes Bowling Alley and Tavern** (6918 St. Clair Ave.) is one. Bowling a set (or do they call it a frame?) at Maple Lanes is like singing a few bars at Carnegie Hall or hitting some pop flies at Fenway. It's a historic spot with real maple-wood lanes, manually operated pin setting machines and ball returns, and scorecards with pen and paper, not overhead projection.

Modern alleys with laminate lanes provide today's bowlers with smooth, even surfaces. The old Maple Lanes, on the other hand, have alleys that have divots and waves in the wood, requiring a bowler to understand the lay of the lane. Current owner of

Maple Lanes Barb Rogers recalls that her father used to say that bowling at Maple Lanes required challenging the lanes, not other bowlers. After over seven decades of play, no player is known to have ever scored the elusive three hundred game.

The front tavern is nearly as compelling a reason to go. A painting of burlesque dancer Lili St. Cyr gazes down at bowlers or drinkers from above the stuck-in-yesteryear bar. The story is that a regular patron of the bar painted Lili's portrait from his memory of her show in Vegas. This was in 1954. His compensation was a six-pack of beer.

Freeway Lanes of Parma (12859 Brookpark Rd.) has forty-two lanes and all the trappings of a prototypical bowling alley, including Wednesday night bowling leagues and Saturday night Cosmic bowling. Cosmic bowling is a new-ish trend using laser lights, disco lights, and black lights. Freeway also has regular live bands.

Twin Lanes Bowling Alley (1812 E. 30th St.) is a timeworn alley run by aging twins, Tim and Tom Menge. They have struggled with the changing neighborhood around them. At times it has been rumored to be closing. For a while it did close Sundays through Tuesdays. Twin Lanes has now returned seven days a week, noon till 10 p.m. except on Fridays and Saturdays, which are noon till midnight. Regardless of the hours, Tim and Tom continuously complain that bowling is to blame for every problem in their life: their weight, their single status, their lack of higher education, and their being broke. "People tell us, 'Man, you got the bowling alley from the '60s. It's like stepping back in time,'" says Tom. "That's fine, but it don't pay the bills."

CHAPTER SEVEN

The Literary Landscape of the Land

WHAT TO READ & WHERE TO GET IT

I think you can find all the elements that you can find in great
literature in mundane experiences.   —*Harvey Pekar*

OST CITIES HAVE THEIR SIGNATURE NOVEL. IN NEW ORLEANS,
it's John Kennedy Toole's *A Confederacy of Dunces.*
For St. Louis it's *The Twenty-Seventh City* by Jonathan Franzen.
In larger cities, you could start a fight (that being a literary fight,
where it'll be punctuation not punches) naming THE most repre-
sentative novel. In Chicago, is it *The Jungle,* or the *Studs Lonigan*
trilogy, or any number of books by Saul Bellow? New York has
literally hundreds. *The Bonfire of the Vanities, Underworld,* and
The Amazing Adventures of Kavalier and Clay seem to top most
current lists. Historically, *The Great Gatsby* and *The Age of Inno-
cence* have to be included. But *Breakfast at Tiffany's, Lush Life,
The Fortress of Solitude, Last Exit to Brooklyn,* and so many more
have their passionate advocates.

If I had to advocate for one for Cleveland, it'd be *Crooked River
Burning* by Mark Winegardner. Mark was born in Bryan, Ohio, a
town once fought over between Ohio and Michigan in the Toledo

War of 1835. Bryan, Ohio, is the current home of Etch A Sketch and Dum Dum Suckers. Winegardner taught a brief while at John Carroll University in Cleveland, now teaches at Florida State, and makes good money doing new books in Mario Puzo's Godfather series. But before he left the area for more frequent sun and better paydays, he soaked in enough impressions to write what *The New York Times* called the "bulky yet brilliant" novel of Cleveland. *Crooked River Burning* is the six-hundred-page love story of the mismatched David Zielinsky, a West Sider from a union family, and Anne O'Connor, an East Side girl whose father is a political boss. Weaving in and out of their story, the novel paints a grand portrait of every aspect of Cleveland's culture: rock 'n' roll, civil rights, labor strikes, organized crime, and pro sports.

Dan Chaon is not from Cleveland. He's from Nebraska, but he currently lives in Cleveland Heights and teaches at Oberlin College. His writing has won awards like the Pushcart Prize and the O. Henry Award, and it has been included in the Best American Short Stories. He was awarded the 2006 Academy Award in Literature from the American Academy of Arts and Letters, and he was nominated for the National Book Award.

Chaon's Cleveland-set novel, *Ill Will*, is brilliant, but filled with cancer, heroin addiction, parricide, and satanic cults—it's rather dark to be a city's signature novel.

Michael Ruhlman, author, home cook, and entrepreneur, is among Cleveland's most prolific writers, having written twenty-one books. He's stacked up *New York Times* bestsellers and James Beard Award winners. He mostly writes about food, including some wonderfully focused books like *Egg: A Culinary Exploration of the World's Most Versatile Ingredient* and *The Book of Schmaltz: A Love Song to a Forgotten Fat*, but also fiction, *In Short Measures*, and a memoir that should be required reading for anyone interested in Cleveland, *House*.

Speaking with Suzanne DeGaetano, the delightful owner of Mac's Backs, she advocated for *Though the Windshield* by

Mike DeCapite. It's one of *those* books. It is treasured by people who have read it, and they treasure the experience all the more because most people have not read it, have not even heard of it.

Fans of *Through the Windshield* bond as sort of a secret society, as do fans of Fred Exley's *A Fan's Notes*.

The novel is about a year in the life of a down-and-out cab driver. Hunks of the work-in-progress were circulated in manuscript form and excerpted in little magazines. It had the reputation of a below-the-radar, underground classic before it was ever published.

Cleveland book reviewer Frank Green called it "a kind of ghost book, disembodied but with a variegated voice that wailed through an underground tunnel connecting literary subcultures."

Making my personal list would be *The Irish Hungarian Guide to the Domestic Arts*. It's Erin O'Brien's food memoir, and I think it should be as well known and often read as *Julie & Julia* or Calvin Trillin's food memoirs except . . . she's from Cleveland and not New York. Spending some time with her, she's as Cleveland as Cleveland gets, a passionate advocate for the weirder parts of the city—much of my "Squaw Rocks!" chapter was created from her leads. Erin is remarkably plugged in to the city as former editor of *Fresh Water Cleveland* and the author of her ongoing personal blog, *The Owner's Manual for Human Beings*.

Her book has been praised as "written by the redheaded, bastard child produced in an unholy union between Erma Bombeck and Hunter S. Thompson. Put simply, O'Brien kicks ass."

Terry Pluto, a sportswriter for *The Plain Dealer*, has written twenty-seven books about sports and four books about his faith. He deserves mention here because several of his books, like *When All the World Was Browns Town* and *The Curse of Rocky Colavito*, do tap into the heart and soul of what it means to be a Clevelander.

Scott Raab, a self-professed "fat Jew from Cleveland, a great deli town," tapped deeply into Cleveland's ravaged heart and soul when he published *The Whore Of Akron: One Man's Search for the Soul Of LeBron James*, after the Chosen One chose to leave Cleveland for Miami. He's penned a less outraged update, *You're Welcome, Cleveland: How I Helped LeBron James Win a Championship for Cleveland.*

Raab is a long time expat, living in New Jersey. But he remains full Cleveland with a Chief Wahoo tattoo, and he carries in his wallet the ticket stub from the 1964 Browns championship game. He was then twelve years old. I was ten and have since lost my ticket and game program.

Cleveland-born and Cleveland-grown Andy Borowitz is rapidly ascending to David Sedaris–like superstar status. He has written several parodies: *The Trillionaire Next Door: The Greedy Investor's Guide to Day Trading, Who Moved My Soap?: The CEO's Guide to Surviving in Prison, Governor Arnold: A Photodiary of His First 100 Days in Office, The Republican Playbook*, and the reviewer-loved memoir *An Unexpected Twist*, about a blockage in his colon that nearly killed him.

Andy is best known for his online posts. He has blogged for the *Huffington Post*. His weekly feature, The Borowitz Report, was a series of Twitter posts chosen as number-one in the world by *Time* magazine. *The New Yorker* acquired the Borowitz Report in 2012 and skyrocketed him to notoriety during the 2016 election cycle. *The Washington Post* called Borowitz "America's finest fake-news creator and sharpest political satirist." The *New York Times* wrote, "Andy Borowitz is the funniest human on Twitter, and that's not mean praise."

Another Clevelander not often thought of as a Clevelander, in fact not often thought of at all, is Michael Weldon. I'm not even sure his book, *The Psychotronic Encyclopedia of Film*, is still in print. During my thirteen years working for Random House/Ballantine and selling books by Norman Mailer, John Irving, Amy Tan, J. R. R. Tolkien, Margaret Atwood, John Updike, Barbara Tuchman, and I could go on, one of my favorite of our publications was *Psychotronic*.

It was a completely eccentric book with Michael's salivating reviews of more than three thousand of the weirdest movies ever made, from *Abbott and Costello Meet Frankenstein* to *Zombies on Broadway*. Included were schlocky horror movies like *Attack of the Crab Monsters* (even the video case for the movie states, "Not as good as you remember it") and *I Dismember Mama*, as well as sexplotation movies *Love Slaves of the Amazon* and *Let Me Die a Woman*. My favorite, understated movie title was *The Creature Wasn't Nice*.

Michael Weldon's writing is so clearly Cleveland. There is no doubt this was a boy who grew up on a steady diet of Ghoulardi. Weldon's bio states, "The author of this book has been watching these movies obsessively since the age of six. He is now unfit for conventional employment."

If there is anyone Cleveland currently considers their bard, it's probably mystery writer Les Roberts. Les grew up in Chicago, spent twenty-four years in LA as a producer and writer for *Hollywood Squares*, *The Andy Griffith Show*, and *The Man from U.N.C.L.E.* His first book, *An Infinite Number Of Monkeys*, was an LA-based mystery. For his next book, his editor wanted the setting moved away from Los Angeles. Roberts went out to find a different setting and chose Cleveland. To me, that stinks of opportunism.

I'm sure I just annoyed a number of people. Les is the recipient of the Cleveland Arts Prize for Literature and has been voted "Cleveland's Favorite Author" by cleveland.com. He now does live in Cleveland Heights. He came to Cleveland to create the lottery game TV show *Cash Explosion Double Play*. The one and only book of his I did read was *Pepper Pike*. I grew up in Pepper Pike. The entire time, I felt like Les was still sitting in Los Angeles with a Cleveland street atlas by his side. Other than getting the street names right, *Pepper Pike* was nothing like Pepper Pike.

When his private eye, Milan Jacovich, stopped into a speakeasy on Chagrin Boulevard, I leapt from my chair. There are no speakeasies on Chagrin Boulevard! It's all strip malls and a Heinen's Grocery Store, where soccer moms ruthlessly cut in line so they won't be late for their tennis lessons. Speakeasies!

When Les scripted a femme fatale living on Gates Mills Boulevard, I again bolted upright. The femme fatales on Gates Mills Boulevard would ensnare the unsuspecting dupe with promises of mind-blowing espresso rather than sex and then place the guy in perilous situations like popping into a Starbucks with her frequent shopper card running a negative balance.

Maybe if I started with his other settings with which I had less affinity, like *Deep Shaker* or *Ashtabula Hat Trick*, I wouldn't have been angered. However, I will always be indignant reading what Les said, "The city reminds me so much of my hometown that I call it Chicago light." Chicago light? You know where you can shove your deep dish pizza.

Damn Right I'm From Cleveland: Your Guide to Makin' It in America's 47th Biggest City is Mike Polk Jr.'s comedic tribute to the city he so clearly loves, but in a natural way between a man and a city, as God intended. Though, I think that since the book's publication Cleveland has slipped from forty-seventh to fifty-first biggest city.

Mike himself says. "I wrote [the book] over the summer in a haze of Coors Light. I get asked about stuff from the book all the time, and I honestly don't always remember everything I wrote in there."

The heavily designed book, perhaps the first ever completely square-shaped book about Cleveland, reminds me (in the tiniest of ways) of Jon Stewart's *America (The Book)*. Mike himself compared it to *Moby Dick*. He stated his book makes Melville's novel look like "a steaming pile of whale shit."

Belt Publishing launched in 2013 as an online magazine and small press with a focus on the Rust Belt. It is the brainchild of Clevelander Anne Trubek. Belt has published an anthology, *Rust Belt Chic: The Cleveland Anthology*, which collects stories, poems, and essays by Clevelanders. More handy for the visitor, Belt has also published *The Cleveland Neighborhood Guidebook*.

Personally, I also consider Anne an important voice in first spotting, then valuing, and finally trying to hang on to what makes Cleveland *Cleveland*. While destination management companies, tourism bureaus, and slick magazines were ballyhooing Cleveland's downtown development, Trubek said, "I really wanted to have a counterbalance to that. We wanted to pan out, look to the sides, and show other Clevelands, too—to let shine the hidden gems, stop to note the cracked glass, and poke into the shadows of what has been lost."

Like most cities in the US, once great independent bookstores have been turned into food co-ops and hemp clothing stores. In the late '70s, I worked in a bookstore on New York's Fifth Avenue. In a single square-mile area there were then thirty-six bookstores, including two huge Doubledays, the beautiful Beaux Arts–style Scribner's Bookstore, Rizzoli, where the clerks went out of their way to ignore you, Haecker, an art bookstore, Facsimile, an Irish one, and the irreplaceable cultural landmark, the Gotham Book Mart. Today, only one bookstore remains, a Barnes & Noble.

Cleveland's classic bookstore back in the day was Kay's. Kay's was a massive, eccentrically designed, chaotically laid out book lover's dream and/or nightmare. The store has been called "a rust belt mutation of Borges's Library of Babel" or "Lucien's library in the Sandman series, the one that contains every book that was only ever dreamed of or never completed."

On three floors were seemingly most books ever in print. If you pulled a book off the shelf, you suddenly realized there were second and third rows of books shoved behind.

The imperious, blue-haired owner, Rachel Kowan, or Kay, held court behind a grand desk, hovering a few feet from the front door. You felt like you were appearing before Courtroom Ten in the Department of Mysteries if you had to ask for help finding a book.

HARVEY PEKAR

I fully believe that I and most people who live in or are from Cleveland consider the one writer who most "got" the heart and soul of Cleveland to be graphic novel writer Harvey Pekar.

Pekar began publishing *American Splendor* in 1976. He'd been inspired by legendary artist R. Crumb during Crumb's time working in Cleveland for American Greetings. The artist saw something in Harvey's short tales and illustrated the first few.

Pekar's gritty and idiosyncratic stories were somewhat of a revelation, one of the first comic books or graphic novels to abandon superheroes or the ubiquitous cuteness of *Peanuts*, *Family Circus*, and *Beetle Bailey*. It's not overstating the case to claim Harvey Pekar is the comix equal to John Steinbeck or Henry James, the pillars of literary realism.

Harvey was a lower-middle-class laborer who worked his entire life as a file clerk in a V.A. hospital and found his artistic inspiration in telling the tales of Cleveland's working class. One tale was titled, "Awaking to the Terror of the Same Old Day." The first Pekar I ever read was a story about his getting a rain-soaked carpet off an outdoor balcony. And that was it. For me, it was nothing short of an epiphany. That beautifully banal story led me to feverishly consume his other tales of the drawn character of Harvey, which covered his interactions with coworkers trying to sell homemade pickles, his car troubles, his money issues, or the existential angst of trying to choose the quickest checkout line in the grocery store.

Pekar produced seventeen issues of *American Splendor*. All were illustrated by others, a long list of noted comic book artists from R. Crumb to Gary Dunn, Dean Haspiel, Drew Friedman, and Rick Geary.

His "big break" came as a guest on David Letterman's show. Letterman undoubtedly saw Harvey Pekar as another in the show's collection of authentic eccentrics like Larry "Bud" Melman, Dick Assman, and Mujibur and Sirajul.

The Pekar-Letterman made-for-TV marriage was short-lived. In his very first appearance, Harvey set the stage by firing off his salvo, "I ain't no showbiz phony." Over several appearances, Cleveland's curmudgeon broke away from the character David desired, replacing Dave as the emblem of a quirky coolness. Letterman was seeming more and more like the uncool former Indiana weatherman out of Ball State that he was. Harvey appeared six times on the show before being banned. The final show is one Letterman probably hopes never re-airs. For once, Letterman lost his veneer of cool and was reduced to a mean-spirited bully, calling *American Splendor* a "little Mickey Mouse magazine" and "rainy day fun for boys and girls."

Harvey went back to being the barely known cult figure, the chronicler of Cleveland's commonplace lives, and a file clerk for the V.A.

In the mid-'80s there was an explosion in the book publishing industry. Graphic novels *Batman: The Dark Knight Returns* and *The Watchmen* became unexpected and huge best sellers. Publishers saw this as the new and major growth area, and many publishing houses went out looking for material to jump on the bandwagon. We all learned that the new trend was just *Batman: The Dark Knight Returns* and *The Watchmen*.

During this time, I called Harvey Pekar to try to lure him to my company. He responded, "I'm a file clerk. I've made peace with that. Leave me alone."

Harvey Pekar died July 12, 2010, of an accidental overdose of antidepressants. Harvey made a career writing about his depressions. He had recently been diagnosed with a return of his cancer. LeBron James had just announced he was taking his talents to South Beach. There were more than enough reasons to feel the need for extra meds.

His wife, Joyce Brabner, got through it all with a display of resilience and black comedy, characteristic of Harvey, characteristic of Cleveland. She claimed to be looking for an appropriate spot on the streets of Cleveland to spread his ashes. Joyce remarked, "He now just looks like kitty litter." When a reporter called for an interview, she responded, "He's still dead. When he comes back, rolls away the rock, I'll let you know."

John Backderf, better known as Derf, is a Clevelander who carries on the Pekar tradition. He sold his first cartoon, a nude portrait of his sixth grade teacher, for $2 dollars to a classmate who used it for unspeakable purposes. Derf went on to create his comic strip, *The City*, which appeared in over 140 publications. *Trashed, Punk Rock & Trailer Parks* was his first graphic novel. *My Friend Dahmer* became an international best seller.

An art school drop out, then garbage collector, Derf has gone on to win numerous awards such as the Angoulême Prize in France, the prestigious Robert F. Kennedy Journalism Award, plus nominations for the Harvey, Ignatz, and Rueben awards, as well as and two Eisner Awards. The latter is sort of the Oscars for graphic novels.

Her responses were legendary. She might say, "Second floor, top shelf on the left, next to a copy of *Journey to Ixtlan*," or, "No. We sold our last copy June 12th last year." Kay *knew* her store.

When you came back to her desk to buy a book, she sometimes told you the price on the cover was wrong and scribbled the new and higher price in black crayon, defacing the book you were just about to buy.

If Kay intimidated you, as she did many, you might wait for her to take a break. Then, her longtime assistant, Harry Condiles, would assume the position at the grand desk. Harry was an elderly, overweight man who had little education but put on the airs of an Ivy League college professor. His image was undercut on the days when he wore shirts with the sleeves cut off, which was often.

In 1983, when Kay had her first year ever in the red, she closed the store. She gave each employee $100 for each year they worked at the store. Harry got $3000. Gary Dunn, who would become better known as an illustrator for many comix, including Harvey Pekar's, got $1600.

Cleveland's bookstores, circa right now, feature **Loganberry Books** (13015 Larchmere Blvd.). Harriet Logan opened the store in 1994. The bookstore has a feature I quite like called "Stump the Bookseller." If you can offer more than "The cover was blue," the Loganberry staff will try to track down your favorite, more or less forgotten book. Unsolved trackings are posted on their website, such as this one: "I'm looking for a book about a man and his dog. The story is told from the dog's perspective. The man also has a hen who loses her toes to frostbite. Not much to go on, but it's all I remember."

Mac's Backs-Books on Coventry (1820 Coventry Rd.) has replaced the Coventry Books of my longhaired and bell-bottomed youth. Coventry Books was where I used to buy all my Alan Watts and Richard Brautigan books. They closed in the early '80s. Mac's Backs-Books restored the tradition of catering to their "hippie"

Mac's has three floors of new and used books

community with alternative literature and many readings held downstairs, while popular graphic novels and science fiction are upstairs.

The well traveled Mac's Backs first opened as a used bookstore in Chagrin Falls back in 1978, then moved to Kent, then back to Chagrin, then to Coventry in '82. The first Coventry location was above the Dobama Theater, then the store moved again to the north end of Coventry for more space, then a third time in 1993 to the location where they've stayed the last twenty-five years.

According to owner Suzanne DeGaetano, Mac's Backs has survived where so many bookstores have failed because it remains a reflection of the area. While they'll carry current hot poets like Nick Flynn and August Kleinzahler (if poets can ever be called "hot"), they remain a place you will still find Gregory Corso and Sylvia Plath.

Their poetry readings, held the second Wednesday of the month, are going on thirty years, making them one of the longest-running reading series in the country. The second Saturday of each month, they host a book club on fiction, fantasy, and adventure for middle-school-aged girls. And there's a nature writers' workshop on the second Friday of each month. "Events are a big part of our identity," DeGaetano said. "It's what we love to do, and it's a way to be part of the community."

Appletree Books (12419 Cedar Rd.) an independent bookstore established in 1975, has passed through three owners. Lynn Quintrell and Alice Webster are the current owners. They have a fine collection of books and also display a commitment to sidelines. Appletree's website announces they are pleased to carry sixteen, mostly local brands of notecards and calendars, plus "literary" candles.

Fireside Bookshop (29 N. Franklin St., Chagrin Falls) was a bookstore I never went to growing up, even though it was located fifteen minutes from my house. I was being a cool (snotty) kid who willfully ignored Fireside Bookshop, because I viewed it as a cutesy suburban bookseller where Mumsie and Nana would take a few hours away from bridge club to buy a nearly word-free picture book about the covered bridges of Ohio. I imagined Fireside would never stock "real" writers like my then-heroes Walter Abish, Alain Robbe-Grillet, and John Fowles. I formed these opinions, of course, having never set foot inside the store.

I did step inside Fireside Bookshop for the first time as a sixty-three-year-old on my return trip. They did have a book by Chuck Palahniuk and one copy of one book by Jonathan Safran Foer, both writers ever so slightly edgy. I didn't see any picture books of the covered bridges of Ohio. But I did find a good ten to twenty one-thousand-piece puzzles of the Chagrin waterfalls.

Horizontal Books (1921 W. 25th St.) is steps from the West Side Market. Ignore the completely empty storefront windows and focus on the (much needed) sign reading, "Yes We're OPEN." Horizontal Books has every-day sales: buy one book and get a 50 percent discount, two books at 60 percent off, and three books 70 percent. They also offered a coupon where if you spent $7, you'd receive a $15 voucher. I sense there is some point at which if you buy enough books, they'll just give you the store.

CHAPTER EIGHT

Squaw Rocks!

EXPLORING THE LAND

Our happiest moments as tourists always seem to come when we stumble upon one thing while in pursuit of something else.

—*Lawrence Block*

ROWING UP, MY FAVORITE SPOTS TO EXPLORE IN CLEVELAND included the Health Museum, which was America's first when it opened in 1940. They had an eighteen-foot-high molar you could walk through and around. The bigger attraction was Juno, a life-size statue of a woman who talked in a recorded voice about the human body and its systems. Her twenty major organs would light up in succession during her chat.

Juno was the first woman I ever saw with absolutely no clothes on. Of course, the fact that she was also transparent and had no visible skin made Juno a bit less sexy. But don't think I and every other third-grade boy weren't envisioning her with a coating of flesh covering up her lungs, internal thoracic artery, and her xiphoid process. I had a childhood friend who painted his clear plastic Visible Woman model kit in flesh tone and then tossed out the plastic bones and organs that didn't align with his third-grade perversions.

I checked Amazon.com, and you can still buy Visible Woman

and Visible Man model kits for about $20. You might first see if you can buy the kits from Big Fun. On Amazon, I also saw the "customers who bought this item also bought" suggestion of a model set of six male prostate glands for $54. They looked like plastic chicken nuggets. Who would buy that?

Juno first appeared in Cleveland on November 13, 1950, but she was actually created in the 1920s by Franz Tschaikart for the German Hygiene Museum. The Cleveland Health Museum paid $15,000 to bring Juno to The Land. She looked headed for a plastic graveyard when the original Health Museum was torn down in 2006. Thankfully, the Dittrick Museum (profiled later in this chapter) saved her after years stuffed inside a packing crate and reintroduced Juno in 2011.

Squire's Castle was another childhood haunt, this one where I refused to go on my return trip while writing this book. It was already a disappointment as a kid. I imagine it'd be an even bigger "That's IT?" through the eyes of an adult.

Squire's Castle wasn't really a castle, but rather intended as a gatehouse and caretaker's quarters for a much larger estate that never got built. The owner wasn't really a nobleman or knight, but Fergus B. Squire, a vice president for Standard Oil. Fergus planned to erect two other large buildings in the style of English baronial halls, but chose instead to build his country estate in Wickliffe. The city of Wickliffe now calls itself "The Gateway to Geauga County," reminding us once again that nicknames should be given by others and never self-imposed. Their slogan implies there's something grand on the other side of that gateway, something bigger like "Gateway to the West" or "Gateway to Hell," and not just gateway to the annual Maple Festival held each April.

Growing up, I spent too many Sunday afternoons at Squire's Castle, joined by hundreds of other kids bored out of their minds, having stopped by the hollowed-out stone structure as part of the family's leisurely drive in the country.

Cleveland has another castle where, quite frankly, I have never been. **Franklin Castle** (4308 Franklin Blvd.) is claimed to be Cleveland's most haunted house. I wasn't afraid of going there, I just never heard of Franklin Castle until writing this book.

It is a large, looming building with thick stone walls and twenty-one rooms, including a turret, wine cellars, numerous hidden passageways, and a fourth-floor ballroom accessible by its own hidden staircase. The whole place has a sinister vibe. Hans Tiedemann, a German immigrant, built the house in the mid-1800s. The Franklin Castle has been used as a meeting place for a German Singing Society, a German Socialist organization, and as a doctor's office, and at one time it housed bootleggers.

There's a gaggle of ghost stories associated with "The Frank." In a small room at the rear of the house a pile of baby skeletons was claimed to have been discovered, supposedly the victims of a sinister or merely inept doctor. "They" say today that babies can still be heard crying in the walls. "They" also claim that a mass killing occurred on the premises when some Nazis inside the house were machine-gunned to death in a political dispute. Throughout the house you can still hear disembodied voices speaking in German. "Was zum scheiße machen wir in Cleveland?" Translation: "What the fuck are we doing in Cleveland?"

Haunted Cleveland Ghost Tours (hauntedcleveland.net) can take you there. I chose not to go because I found their fee, $52, a bit scary.

While my Health Museum is gone and my description of Squire's Castle probably won't cause you to rush there, **Squaw Rock** beckons. Squaw Rock sits in the middle of the South Chagrin Reservation Park.

The bas-relief sculpture, carved into a massive riverside boulder, is of a woman, maybe naked up top (at least that's what third-grade boys liked to imagine), wearing funky yoga or exercise-style shorts, with something like a Batman cape flowing behind her. She is encircled in the sculpted oddity by a huge twenty-foot snake, a dead lion or deer or dog to the side (the sculpture is sort of naive art, i.e., can't really tell what it is), an axe in the lower left corner, and I think that's a baby in a papoose in the lower right. The whole presentation has this floating-in-space feel to it like a Chagall painting. As kids, we ran with that name, Squaw Rock, and held to the belief that it was carved by ancient Indians. It was actually executed by blacksmith turned self-taught artist Henry Church in 1885.

BTW, for third-grade girls there is the equal of Juno and Squaw Rock. On the front of the National City Bank Building, on the northeast corner of East 6th Street and Euclid Avenue, is a high-up sculpted male nude in desperate need of a fig leaf. He's known as Downtown's Naked Man.

For the rest of this chapter, my conceit and willful arbitrariness will not profile more common places like the zoo or the Rock & Roll Hall of Fame. I'd rather devote my time and your reading diversion to places like the **Percy Skuy Collection on the History of Contraception**. Percy was a marketing man for Ortho Pharmaceutical. His professional focus was contraceptives and gynecological care. He began amassing contraceptive devices in 1965.

The collection evolved into a traveling mini-museum in his suitcase. Eventually, he stockpiled so much stuff, he needed a permanent home far larger than his suitcase. Today, the Percy Skuy Collection is on permanent display at the **Dittrick Museum of**

Medical History (11000 Euclid Ave.). Today, his stuff is over one thousand items. The collection contains beaver testicles, cat bones, ear wax from a mule, deer skins, Mexican yams, formaldehyde powder, rubbers made by Goodyear Tires, rhythm beads, dates, honey, sponges, diaphragms, loops, pills, and IUDs, all displayed in a chronological tribute to pre–Planned Parenthood attempts to not get pregnant.

The museum also maintains a collection of historical writings of how people dealt with avoiding pregnancy centuries ago. There's nothing so effective as the ancient Egyptian method from 1850 B.C.: Crocodile shit was used as a suppository. Seriously. In more recent enlightened times, a lemon wedge was used as a cervical cap and lemon juice as a spermicide. You probably winced reading that, just as I winced writing it.

The Dittrick Museum is more than just a world-class collection of contraceptives. It also houses many other historical oddities of medicine, like a comprehensive collection of surgical instruments, artifacts related to bloodletting, beautiful old microscopes, and nursing uniforms from throughout history. That collection will allow you to imagine what young women wore to Halloween parties in the early 1900s when they wanted to go as a sexy nurse.

Cleveland's Art Museum or Museum of Natural History are both quite good but offer little more than what you'd expect. Well, I might dabble in the **Natural History Museum** (1 Wade Oval Dr.) for a minute to see the taxidermic body of Balto the Sled Dog. He was the heroic sled dog of Nome, Alaska. In 1925, the city was hit with an outbreak of diphtheria. The antidote was miles away in Anchorage and unable to be reached by plane because of miserable weather. Balto, a Siberian Husky, led his team of sled dogs through whiteout conditions and temperatures forty degrees below zero.

Cleveland Museum of Natural History, east of downtown

He was heralded as a hero. A statue of Balto was placed in Central Park in New York. A two-reel documentary film called *Balto's Race to Nome* was made, although no prints remain. More recently, Amblin Entertainment released a cartoon version in 1995.

However, his fame faded, and he and the other sled dogs became a vaudeville sideshow, eventually kenneled inside a Los Angeles dime museum. George Kimble, a Cleveland businessman, found them barely cared for and raised $2000 in pre–GoFundMe days to buy Balto and his fellow sled dogs. He brought the dogs to Cleveland, where they lived in relative comfort at the zoo. After Balto died in 1933, his body was taxidermied and stands in the museum.

The **Museum of Contemporary Art Cleveland, or MOCA** (11400 Euclid Ave.), is also kind of cool, particularly the building itself, designed by Iranian-born, London-based Farshid Moussavi. The striking six-sided facility looks like a gigantic chunk of a shiny mineral, some sides triangular, some trapezoidal.

Inside, the artwork is almost trumped by the weird fire escape staircase, called Stair A. The stairs twist and turn, painted bright yellow, and with disorienting music piped in. I'd say "don't trip" but I think trippiness is rather the point.

The museum I'd rush to is the **Museum of Divine Statues** (12905 Madison Ave.). With Cleveland's declining population and even more rapid decline in churchgoers, the Catholic Diocese announced the wholesale closing of fifty churches in 2009. Many Catholics and non-Catholic alike were distraught at the idea of all the statues of angels and saints being destroyed. Not twenty feet from me right now, I have a five-foot plaster statue of Jesus with the sacred heart. I bought it from a church that was going to be torn down.

Louis McClung stepped up to save Cleveland's statuary. He took over one of the abandoned churches, St. Hedwig's to create the Museum of Divine Statues. Opened in 2011, McClung has a mission to rescue and restore some of those icons. Consider it a homeless shelter for abandoned statues.

A former professional makeup artist, McClung repaints and restores the statues back to their original splendor. The first thing he did was to gut the church. "It was all 1970s and gross," Lou said. "There was no way I was gonna roll like that." He salvaged stained-glass windows and architectural bits from other closed parishes and installed them in his museum. Then he placed each restored statue in an individual pool of light. St. Sebastian's dripping blood was never so resplendent. St. Lucy's tray of eyeballs never so incandescent. The perfect lighting and pumped-in music makes Lou's museum a true treasure.

When first considering his museum, he said, "Some people thought I was frickin' crazy." His use of the past tense implies, perhaps erroneously, that people no longer consider it frickin' crazy.

Another statue worth visiting, this one not housed in a museum, is the Harvey Pekar statue on the second floor of the **Cleveland Heights–University Heights Library** (2345 Lee Rd.). The Harvey bronze statue stands only two and a half feet high, depicting him shrugging his shoulders as he steps out of one of his graphic novel pages. A dialogue bubble for little Harvey reads, "Oy vey! What do you want from my life?"

The city has also approved a thirteen-foot stainless steel statue of the Man of Steel. Superman was born in Cleveland in 1933 by writer Jerry Siegel and artist Joe Shuster, both high school students at Glenville High. They were so poor at the time, the two created the panels on the back of old wallpaper sheets. The childhood homes where Siegel (10622 Kimberly Ave.) and Shuster

Great Lakes Science Center on the shore of Lake Erie

(10905 Amor Ave.) grew up both have commemorative markings on the fences and front porches.

Lakewood artist David Deming may have his statue of Superman gracing the Lakefront when you visit. The design was approved in 2015. The space has been chosen, at the base of a new Lakefront bridge, in between the Rock & Roll Hall of Fame and the Great Lakes Science Center. Now Deming just needs to build the statue and then undergo the rigorous process of city and county design reviews and safety regulations.

When you can actually visit the statue is anyone's guess. A model stands inside the Public Library main branch. The library also has Jerry's boyhood desk, where the comics were created, and an exhibit of about seventeen thousand pieces of Superman memorabilia, donated by Arkansas native Mike Curtis.

Clevelanders seem to have mixed feelings about the giant sculpture of the **World's Largest Rubber Stamp** (Lakeside Ave., two blocks from the Rock & Roll Hall of Fame). Some feel honored that internationally famous Pop artist Claus Oldenburg graced the city with one of his pieces. He has forty-four oversized sculptures of everyday objects spread across the globe. Others look at it with their most disdainful WTF expressions. The Hastily Made Cleveland Tourism video described the stamp as follows: "We're so retarded, we think this is art."

Standard Oil of Ohio commissioned Oldenburg to create the twenty-eight-foot tall, forty-eight-foot long office stamp in 1985. It was intended to be placed in front of their headquarters on Euclid Avenue, but when Standard Oil was acquired by BP, the new CEO, Robert Horton, didn't want the word FREE, as used on the stamp, displayed anywhere associated with his company. So, the piece sat for seven years in a warehouse in Whiting, Indiana.

Eventually, to get it out of their warehouse and off their hands,

The Big Stamp. Not pictured: the Big Pencil

the company offered to donate the sculpture to Cleveland as public art. The city refused. The company counter offered to ship and install for FREE—and the rest is a footnote in the history of The Land.

Oldenburg also intended to build a large-scale arch in the shape of a bent screw to be placed in front of the Frank J. Lausche State Office Building. Concerned about a large art installation that looked like a limp penis, the city rejected this one before it got further than a few sketches.

In addition to the Big Stamp, Cleveland has the **Big Pencil**. Across from a branch of the Cleveland Museum of Art (intersection of W. 29th St. and Church St.), an old metal pipe has been turned into a No. 2 pencil.

Keith Haring, another internationally famous artist, had his bright orange and blue **Acrobat** placed near the entrance of the Glennan Building by Van Horn Field on the campus of Case Western University.

The Politician: A Toy (East 18th St. and Chester Ave.) is an equally peculiar piece of public art. It was created in 1995 by artist Billie Lawless. It looks like the Disney character Panchito Pistoles as if rendered by Pablo Picasso and stuck in a wheel chair. The sculpture stands over forty feet tall, with wheels that cause a beak to open and close.

Here too, the sculpture raised a bit of controversy. Cleveland mayor Michael R. White opposed *The Politician* being erected simply because he thought it was ugly. Displaying more transparency than most public officials, Mayor White directly stated, "I've seen it and I don't like it."

Lawless got a permit and placed the sculpture on a private lot at East 66th Street and Chester Avenue. When the land was put up for sale in 2008, the sculpture was dismantled, repaired, and moved to the Cleveland State University campus, where it remains today.

While clearly a tourist attraction (it draws 400,000 visitors a year), the **Lake View Cemetery** (12316 Euclid Ave.) is a Cleveland classic and one of the more noted cemeteries in the country.

Your visit will be best served by picking up a map at the cemetery office or online (www.gfdstudios.com/lakeview/media/lake-view-map.pdf).

Founded in 1869, Lake View Cemetery is the final respite for more than 100,000 Clevelanders. Famous residents include an impossible-to-miss, massive (180 feet tall) sandstone building that houses the remains of President James A. Garfield. Around

Lake View Cemetery, the final destination for many Clevelanders

the exterior are five terra-cotta panels with 110 carved figures, all life-size, depicting the events of Garfield's life.

The building combines Romanesque, Gothic, and Byzantine styles of architecture. Inside are gold mosaics, stained-glass windows, and a statue of the President sculpted by Alexander Doyle. You can climb up sixty-four steps from the lobby to the outdoor balcony to capture one of the best views of the Lake Erie shoreline.

The cemetery has a memorial marker to the "Untouchable" crime fighter Eliot Ness, though his ashes were actually scattered in a small pond on the grounds. Next to Eliot Ness's marker lies another Cleveland legend, creative curmudgeon Harvey Pekar. His simple grave is carved with a Harvey quote: "Life is about women, gigs, an' bein' creative."

If you visit John D. Rockefeller's grave, you're supposed to leave dimes at the base of his hard-to-miss, seventy-foot obelisk (and I did). This is a tribute to Rockefeller's habit of giving away shiny

Lincoln Park: a peaceful spot in the middle of Tremont

new dimes during the Great Depression. While he mostly gave dimes to children, he spread the wealth, one time giving a dime to a fellow millionaire, tire magnate Samuel Firestone. The story is he passed out $35,000 in nothing but dimes.

Also buried in Lakeview are the brothers Otis and Mantis Van Sweringen. They're barely known to residents, but they were hugely influential in creating the city. They used part of their 1,400-acre land holdings to convert what was a home for the North Union Community of the Society of Believers (better known as the Shakers) into the planned garden community with tree-lined curved roads rather than the typical grid pattern. This would become Shaker Heights. Then, to give the community easy access to downtown, they created a streetcar line, the Rapid Transit. Then, they purchased land in the vicinity of Public Square to provide a terminus for their rapid transit line. This would become the Terminal Tower.

In addition to creating three of Cleveland's landmarks, the two also well represent Cleveland simply by being just a little bit weird. They never married, slept in same bedroom in their fifty-four room mansion, and were rarely seen in public and never except together. The brothers are buried together in Lakeview Cemetery under a tombstone that reads, "Brothers."

Raymond Johnson Chapman's grave is another easy one to spot. He was the only MLB player to be killed by a pitch. The Indians shortstop died when hit on the temple by a Yankees pitcher. The team dedicated the rest of its 1920 season to Chapman and beat the Brooklyn Dodgers for Cleveland's first (of only two) World Series victories.

Chapman's grave jumps out because of the cluster of balls, bats, and baseball caps left there by the surprising number of people who seem to know his story. Or, maybe it's one guy who comes every other day.

Other graves of note include George Coates Ashmun, who served as a personal bodyguard to President Lincoln. After the little incident at Ford's Theatre, it's hard to claim he was good at his job. But he went on to become a surgeon/teacher in World War I and a professor at Cleveland's Case University.

Also to be found at the cemetery, Garrett A. Morgan Sr. was an African American businessman whom invented the red-yellow-green traffic light and the gas masks used by American soldiers in World War I. Gloria Hershey Pressman appeared in the original *Little Rascals*. Under the stage name Mildred Jackson, she also acted in the film *Moby Dick* with John Barrymore, *The Virginian* with Gary Cooper, and the first talkie, *The Jazz Singer*, with Al Jolson. Dr. James Henry Salisbury was a noted microbiologist and physician. He pioneered research efforts to regarding the link between food and health. He is best known for the Salisbury steak, a curative dietary dish.

Alexander Winton is the "Other Guy" to Henry Ford's "The Guy." Originally a bicycle manufacturer, Winton pioneered Cleveland's automobile industry. In 1897, he drove one of his vehicles to New York in less than ten days, proving the reliability of his new vehicles. The sale of one of his cars in 1898 was the first commercial sale of an American-made, standard-model, gasoline automobile.

The most striking grave marker may be the unsettling statue known as Haserot's Angel. Officially known as "The Angel of Death Victorious," the eerie statue is a well known memorial at the gravesite of the Francis Haserot family. It was created by sculptor Herman Matzen in 1924. The angel of death statue appears to weep black tears. The "tears" formed over time, an effect of the aging bronze.

Away from the cemetery and even more strange than a weeping statue is a large plaque telling the story of the **Land of the Warres** (701 Perkins Ave.). Eames Demetrios is an artist, designer, filmmaker, and brilliantly bizarre TED speaker. He conceptualized Kcymaerxthaere as a "parallel universe that intersects with much of our linear Earth, but with different stories, creatures, peoples, even laws of physics and qualities of existence." His words, not mine.

Demetrios installs copy-heavy markers at locations all over the world, creating real intersections with his imagined universe. His bronze markers are set up in London, Cyprus, Indonesia, Charleston, SC, and New Harmony, Indiana. It's all a bit over my head.

There's another weird tile of questionable history embedded in the asphalt at the intersection of W. Prospect and W. 3rd. The **Cleveland Toynbee Tile** is part of one of a worldwide project with hundreds of similar tiles scattered across the globe. They instruct passers-by to "Resurrect Dead on Planet Jupiter" as part of the "Toynbee Idea." Nobody knows who placed the tiles, which started showing up in the 1980s in Philadelphia.

The **Warner and Swasey Observatory** (1950 Hanover Dr., at N. Taylor), while looking to the stars, is far more earthbound than the Kcymaerxthaere plaque or Toynbee tile.

The original observatory was gifted to the Case School of Applied Science in 1919 by the Warner and Swasey telescope company. Unfortunately, by 1950 the growth of the city resulted in too much ambient light, making the telescope unusable. It was moved to a new location in Arizona. The Taylor Road facility continued to conduct astronomical research into the 1970s, but the site was completely abandoned by 1982.

It is now a shrine to what some next-generation artists love and refer to as "ruin porn." While covered in creeping ivy, and with huge holes in the viewing dome, the long-abandoned building retains a certain grandeur. Rust Belt cities like Detroit, Buffalo, and certainly Cleveland are stocked with once great buildings that used to be factories, churches, and music halls. There are literally tens if not hundreds of websites devoted to the most breathtaking and hauntingly abandoned places. Photographers Matthew Christopher, Anna Mika, and others have made careers of capturing the beauty as nature reclaims man-made edifices.

The fates were not so kind another "ruin porn" shrine to decrepitude, the **Duck Factory**. It was a large abandoned factory at the corner of East 120th Street and Coltman Avenue. In the early part of the twentieth century the building was used for streetcar maintenance. Once streetcars fell out of use, the city sold the building to Woodhill Supply, Inc., a plumbing and tool company. They too moved out in 2011 because maintenance on the old building became too expensive.

For the next four years, the abandoned and increasingly ramshackle property became a favorite spot for photographers or teenagers looking for a cool spot to get pictures or get high. The attraction was not just the big empty space, but that the big empty space was filled with yellow rubber duckies, thousands of them. The duckies were lined up on ledges and arranged in rows; scattered across the factory floors, jammed into former cubbies, peeking out of otherwise empty closets, and seemingly marching up and down old bowed and creaky staircases.

Years ago, a local charity had approached Woodhill to store the toy ducks. The charity used them each Spring for a fund-drive race down the river. People sneaking into the abandoned space found the rubber ducks in storage and starting making duck altars and dioramas throughout the factory.

Tragedy struck on September 27, 2015. A devastating fire swept through the brick building. The cause of the fire was never determined, but authorities suspect "fowl" play.

The Duck Factory is an Ain't There No More. Liberty Row is an Ain't There Depending on the Light of Day. There are nearly **one hundred oak trees** lining South Park Boulevard between North Woodland Road and Warrensville Center Road. The trees have been accessorized since 1919 with a bronze (now oxidized to green) plaque bearing the name of a Clevelander who died in World War I. In certain light, the stretch of trees seems to glow in a seafoam green.

* ★ *

While the next two exploration spots may seem a little like—OK, very much like—touristy spots, the Cleveland Public Library and Playhouse Square have some less obvious reasons to go.

A variety of perks can be viewed at the main branch of the **Cleveland Public Library** (325 Superior Ave.). The library has one of the most extensive collections in the country, boasting close to ten million items. It was the first library in America to allow people to search the shelves for books. Previously, visitors to libraries had to wait while staff members tracked down volumes. But for seekers of (very modest) thrills, they display the biggest collection of chess and checkers sets in the world, miniature books, so small you need a magnifying glass to read them, illuminated manuscripts, and a brick from the Great Wall of China. The library should probably be ashamed of that brick. Nearly one third of the Ming Dynasty–era wall is gone—thanks, in part, to tourists lifting bricks to keep as souvenirs.

Playhouse Square is five theaters and 1.3 million square feet of performance space, making it the largest performing arts center in the United States outside of New York City. They host more than one thousand events and a million people a year.

The Cleveland Play House, founded in 1915, was America's first professional regional theatre. I didn't know that fact until writing

The sign above Playhouse Square

this book. I have told far too many tour-takers in New Orleans that Le Petit Theatre is the oldest. Le Petit was founded a year later, in 1916.

Plans to raze the Ohio and the State Theatres in 1970s caused a public outcry, and the newly formed Playhouse Square Foundation preserved and restored the district. The twenty-foot-tall outdoor chandelier, either glitzy or tastelessly kitschy depending on your taste, is a draw for many. The chandelier was officially declared by Guinness as the largest in the world.

Far fewer know about the **Prop Shop and Prop Storage** (7401 Detour Ave.—yes, that's a real street name). It is not set up for tours nor drop ins, but if you're adventurous, damn charming, and always willing to have the door figuratively slammed in your face, you might try calling to schedule a peek.

The Prop Shop has over eleven thousand square feet of space, filled to the rafters with stage props. Everything from furniture (including fourteen pianos) to plastic chickens and a loaf of plastic challah bread are stored inside. There is a section specifically for taxidermied animals, including a very large moose head from a 1930s production.

The Zero Gravity Research Facility at Cleveland's **NASA Glenn Research Center** (21000 Brookpark Rd.) is the last remnant of the space program in Cleveland and the largest drop tower in the country. It plummets 510 feet underground, or about as deep as the Washington Monument is tall. Scientists suck out all the air in the tower to then drop in pods to study aspects of space flight in a weightless environment. Between 120 and 200 tests a year are conducted here.

In the unlikely event that you'll be allowed in, don't get too close to the edge. A worker actually did fall in once. The fall was bad enough, but at the bottom of the tower are twenty-foot-deep tubes filled with little Styrofoam balls intended to catch and protect the pod. The styrofoam did save his life, but it is like quicksand. Every movement makes you sink deeper, and the little pellets are small enough to inhale. This particular fellow was rescued by being pulled up with an air hose.

I learned about this last place for exploration from Michael Symon in a *Food & Wine* article. **The Schvitz** (E. 116th St. and Luke Ave.) is a rustic bath house in business since the 1920s. *Schvitz* means "to sweat" in Yiddish.

Back then, the area was a thriving neighborhood full of Hungarian immigrants. Today, the Schvitz remains in its original location, but the neighborhood has declined. To get to the Schvitz, you go down a deserted, dead-end alley to a windowless brick building with no posted address. Am I over-hyping so far?

The Schvitz is a steam room/bar/restaurant/private club for men only. When men arrive, many of whom look like they've been out of work since *The Sopranos* went off the air, they head upstairs to get a locker, strip down, and grab a towel. Then, it's down to the steam room to sweat and occasionally nod off while they wait for their name to be called for a massage. The all-male masseurs range from giving a platza, administered with oak leaves, to outright deep-tissue torture.

Outside of the steam room are showers and an unheated pool, most often the water at a manhood-shriveling forty degrees. The strategy is, you emerge sweating from the steam room and then jump directly into the cold pool. This I gather makes crazy paterfamiliae feel most fully alive.

All of this is foreplay to the main event, taking a seat (draped in a towel and little else) inside the dining room, which is spartanly unadorned except for a photograph of General Patton urinating into the Rhine.

The Schvitz provides platters stacked with pickles, peppers, and rye bread, along with beefy slabs of ribeye steaks, infused with more garlic than should be legal.

CHAPTER NINE

I Returned to Cleveland and All I Got Was This Lousy (but Beautiful) Hat

SHOPPING IN CLEVELAND

B ECAUSE SHOPPING IS ALL ABOUT UNCONTROLLED EXCESS (at least when it's fun), here I start the chapter with three quotes, not just one.

Whoever said money can't buy happiness simply
didn't know where to go shopping. —*Bo Derek*

If you think the United States has stood still, who built
the largest shopping center in the world? —*Richard M. Nixon*

Other societies create civilizations; we build shopping malls.
—*Bill Bryson*

For this chapter, I choose not to profile fashion shops, day spas, or cork accessory stores. If you desire these, open up your hotel's *Welcome to Cleveland* guest book or grab a copy of *Cleveland Magazine*. Each is loaded with ads for local shopping experiences like The Dancing Sheep, wearable art, or Ambiance, a store for lovers. I will, instead, highlight eclectic stores. What I discovered when rediscovering Cleveland is that it has more eclectic shops than my beloved New Orleans. With another few months of gentrification and greedy landlords in New York City, Cleveland will have more cool stores than the Big Increasingly Unaffordable Apple.

STUFF TO WEAR

First off, I have got to say that during my return trip, I have never seen more people wearing clothing with native insignia than in Cleveland. You do see the occasional Saints and LSU T-shirts in New Orleans. I used to see Yankees and Giants and Jets wear in New York. But, elsewhere it isn't eight out of ten people covered in logos for the hometown Browns, Indians, and Cavs, or the logos CLE, Believeland, and The Land.

Listed below are some shops to fit in like a local and buy your own Cleveland wear.

Cleveland Clothing Co. uses for their tag line, "Spreading Cleveland Pride One T-Shirt at a Time." They have three locations: 342 Euclid Ave. (Downtown), 11435 Euclid Ave. (University Circle), and 64 SS Comet Lane (Westside), but probably sell most of their wares via their website, cleclothingco.myshopify.com. They also sell accessories like jewelry, stickers, car magnets, bottle openers, and sunglasses. The stores are chosen most every year as "Best T-Shirt Company," "Best Gift Shop," and "Best Place to Buy a Piece of Cleveland" by *Cleveland Magazine* and *Cleveland Scene*. There are T-shirt designs for most every Cleveland nickname except Mistake By the Lake, which wouldn't exactly be spreading the pride. You can buy T-shirts inscribed CLE, Forest City, the Plum, 6th City (now 51st), BelieveLand, and, of course, The Land. In addition to Browns, Indians, Cavs, and Cleveland Rocks! T-shirts, Cleveland Clothing also has a full line of Stipe Miocic wear.

I bought their Joe & Freddie Slyman's T-shirt.

GV Apparel has two retail locations, 17128 Detroit Ave. in Lakewood and 38038 Second St. in Willoughby. Again, most sales are probably through their website, gvartwork.com.

Started in 2009 as a "Cleveland That I Love" campaign, it is the brainchild of George Vlosich III.

His notoriety began as an Etch A Sketch artist. His incredibly detailed art became a YouTube sensation. The video showing him making a LeBron James portrait got a million hits a week.

Each of his original Etch pieces takes him seventy to eighty hours to create. The pieces are preserved so they won't jostle into oblivion, and they've been featured in galleries throughout the world and have sold for more than $10,000.

GV Apparel sells mostly T-shirts, mostly focused on the city's sports teams. My favorite is the "Factory of Sadness" design depicting the Browns' stadium. There are also off-message T-shirt designs showing JFK and Ronald Reagan. Maybe it's part of his yet-unnamed Presidents Who Got Shot collection.

I bought their elegant silver-on-black baseball cap embroidered with "The LAND," where the iconic Terminal Tower violates the letter A.

Only in Clev (17025 Lorain Ave.) sells Cleveland-themed candles, glassware, prints by local artists, wall decals, and socks, but mostly customizable shirts, in addition to Cleveland sports team shirts (my favorite being a fighting Brownie elf). They also have shirts showing Municipal Stadium, the polish boy sandwich, and a shirt inscribed "The Land of the Pierogis."

STUFF TO EAT

The sixty-five-year-old **B.A. Sweetie** (6770 Brookpark Rd.) claims to be the largest candy store in America. Daffin's Chocolate Kingdom in Sharon, PA, and Minnesota's Largest Candy Store in Jordan, MN, might want to argue the point, but it is definitely the largest one in Cleveland.

Whenever you visit, an average 400,000 pounds of over 4,000 different candy items are there to greet you among its eleven extra-wide aisles. Nostalgic candy favorites include Bonomos Turkish Taffy, SloPoke, BB Batts, Kits, Broadway licorice rolls, Pop Rocks, wax lips and fangs, and candy sticks (formerly called candy cigarettes in less PC times).

One wall holds a display of Pez dispensers the store claims is the world's largest. Here, they'll have to fend off similar claims from the Pez Museum in Burlingame, CA.

Lilly Handmade Chocolate (761 Starkweather Ave.) sells artisanal chocolates. In addition to truffles and elegant individual chocolates, they offer massive and crudely cut hunks called Monster Bars. The one called Chomp Monster is black mission figs with roasted salty almonds and dark chocolate. Lilly pairs chocolate with sample portions of craft beer or fine wine for their in-house "Pick and Pour."

Malley's Chocolates has been a Cleveland institution since 1935. They started with a single shop in Lakewood, a combination confectionary and ice cream parlor. The Malley family lived in the back room. There are now twenty-two Malley's across the Cleveland area. I don't believe any of the third-generation Malleys live in the back of the shops. All are decorated in their signature pink and pale green colors.

Their home base (13400 Brookpark Rd.) is a five-acre, sixty-thousand-square-foot factory where all chocolates are made. The factory's three tall silos can be spotted miles away. The pink towers are inscribed Cocoa, Milk, and Sugar.

Your rent-a-car company may object, but if you place a Malley's pink and green "CHOC" sticker on your bumper, you could be spotted and win one of their monthly $500 coupons or several of their on-the-spot $25 giveaways.

Fear's Confection (15208 Madison Ave.) is the newest place for chocolates in The Land. After being laid off from her job as a fiber optic networking engineer, Cassandra Fear went way off course in 2010 and started her new life as a home-based confectioner. Her home was quickly overrun with chocolates and brownies piled onto every flat surface. In 2013, Fear's Confections made a leap of faith to a production and retail space. Handmade in small batches, Fear's offers fifteen types of brownies, plus chocolates, cookies, caramels, toffees, truffles, and a non-Cleveland import from her childhood memories of Buffalo, sponge candy. Some cookies and chocolates are offered in what she calls her Nerd Collections, *Star Wars*– and *Dr. Who*–molded sweets, plus my personal favorite, Krampus bars, for $3 (only available in December). Krampus is a Bavarian legend, a horned figure described as "half-goat, half-demon." During the Christmas season he's the anti-Santa and punishes bad children.

If you've had your fill of chocolates, **Richard's Maple Products** (545 Water St.) in Chardon can satisfy your sweet tooth with maple products. They have been a family business since 1910, offering maple syrup, maple drop candy, maple spreads, maple BBQ sauce and mustard, maple creme cookies, maple jelly, and maple-covered dog bones for your Fido or Buddy back home.

STUFF TO HEAR

The no-longer-in-business Rendezvous Records was one of the most historically important record stores in the country. Cleveland still has dozens of first-rate ones, and it may well be the best city you'll ever visit if you're looking for vinyl. Assaulted by Spotify and Apple Music, most stores have survived through a renewed commitment to vinyl.

Cleveland has a first rate vinyl-pressing plant in **Gotta Groove Records** (3615 Superior Ave.). They do offers tours of the facility for a behind-the-scenes look. Since opening in 2009, Gotta Groove has earned a reputation for being on the cutting edge of vinyl manufacturing for making technicolor records, some with artful "spiral" effects. They have made records with glitter, leaves, pages from a two-hundred-year-old book, and shredded

Loop is a coffeehouse and record store all in one

cash. Their attempt to make a great-smelling record from coffee grounds ended up being a greasy mess, but they are always willing to try new things.

With apologies to Bent Crayon, Nikki's Music, Hausfrau Records, The Loop in Tremont, A Separate Reality (which has over twenty thousand albums), and a host of other great stores in neighboring Akron and Oberlin, I'll highlight just a few.

One of the best stores, **Music Saves** (15801 S Waterloo Rd.) has a black cat named Vinyl as their mascot. Owner and passionate advocate for below the radar music Melanie Hershberger specializes in current, indie rock, and underground music. The store carries mostly new vinyl and CDs, with a small selection of used.

When you enter **Blue Arrow Records & Books** (16001 Waterloo Rd.), you literally walk over some of the greatest music ever. Their floor is covered in famous record covers.

My Mind's Eye (16010 Detroit Ave.) is one of the oldest record stores in town and packed with old and new vinyl records in every corner of the store.

Young King's (1418 W 29th St.), not to be confused with the dive bar Little King's (3061 Payne Ave.), is an emerging Hingetown cultural oasis. The store's passions favor jazz, soul, hip-hop, and funk. They have weekly specials: 10% off used jazz vinyl on Tuesdays, 10% off used R&B vinyl on Wednesdays. They also sponsor a musical pop-up, where DJ Red brings records from the store to spin live tracks at Mahall's Locker Room (13200 Madison Ave.), a restaurant, bar, live music, and bowling venue.

STUFF TO HANG ON THE WALL
OR THROW ON THE FLOOR

Flower Child (11508 Clifton Blvd.) claims to be the region's premier retro vintage shop. Yahoo! Style backs them up by choosing them as one of the twelve best vintage stores in the entire country. Inside a nine-thousand-square-foot space, there are seemingly endless rooms of mid-century kitsch, clothing, decor, and furniture.

Says owner Joe Valenti, "I grew up with Mr. Jingeling and Higbee's and all of those things that were simple and nice. I like to capture those moments and bring them back."

Something Different Gallery (1899 W 25th St.) can't compete with the size and breadth of Flower Child, but their eclectic selection is more focused on local artists, cards, and decor. Plus, the staff are likely to greet you with a glass of complimentary wine.

West of Venus (10024 Lorain Ave.) is named after the hit song of retro group the B-52s.

Throughout the three rooms, furniture, artwork, and collectibles span the entire mid-century, but the shop specializes in 1950s and '60s goods. Among tables and chairs, you can find old cameras, a Magnavox record player, pinball games, Noritake and Mikasa china, and plenty of vinyl records.

Norton Furniture has become a bizarre mainstay in Cleveland mostly because of the bizarre owner, Marc Brown. His late-night TV commercials straddle the line between DIY amateur hour and acid flashbacks. They have aired on fourteen different stations, always between the hours of midnight and 5 a.m. The commercials feature Brown, an elderly man with a long gray ponytail and both a voice and a cadence that'll make you think he just smoked a ton of weed. Actually, he was kicked in the throat as a kid, leaving him sounding like Harvey Fierstein at half speed.

The multi-story furniture store (2106 Payne Ave.) is located in a neighborhood consisting of run-down houses, a homeless shelter, and a sea of Cleveland State University parking lots. He caters to mostly poor people when their ancient couches or beds finally give out. His ubiquitous TV commercials carry the tagline, "If you can't get credit in my store, you can't get credit anywhere."

To back up the TV spots, Norton Furniture uses the lure of fiberglass sculptures throughout the store, depicting celebrities like Ray Charles, Rodney Dangerfield, James Brown, the Blues Brothers, Mike Tyson, Betty Boop, and a wizard. As Brown notes, "Children take their parents here to buy furniture. I want this to be a paradise for children, so they love it and bring their parents back."

Even if you don't get by the store, you owe yourself a view of the YouTube TV commercials.

Moonstruck (11917 Mayfield Rd.) is a vintage recycle and reuse home decor and gift shop. They sell repurposed architectural elements and cool quotes printed on vintage fabrics. The store calls their wares, "One of a kind, well-loved items."

In the 216 (1854-A Coventry Rd.) sells T-shirts, jewelry, glassware, soaps, bead oils, men's ties, women's bags made from record albums, coffee bags, books, old bank bags, postal bags, industrial aprons, glass trees made from recycled glass, signs and wall hangings made from old license plates, one of a kind soft sculptures, mixed media and paintings, all-natural dog treats, dog scarves, dog toys, and paper roses made from Cleveland maps, with the one caveat: "Everything's made right here in the state of Ohio."

Visiting In the 216, I bought coasters imprinted with images of Ghoulardi and Dorothy Fuldheim and made by Foundry Woodprints. They make Cleveland memorabilia where vintage and a few contemporary photos are reproduced on birchwood for a truly unique look. In addition to Ghoulardi and Dorothy Baby, you can buy distressed nostalgic images of the Hough Bakery and Higbee's.

Cleveland in a Box (530 Euclid Ave.) is exactly what it sounds like. You can visit the store or contact them online (info@clevelandinabox.com), choose five to ten Cleveland-centric items, and they ship the box anywhere in the world. Their website states, "We're constantly working with local vendors and merchants to bring you an ever-changing and growing variety of Cleveland essentials."

If you go to the Cleveland in a Box storefront, located in the 5th Street Arcade, you have to take a spin in the Spun Chairs. Located in the common area of the mini-arcade, these Thomas Heatherwick creations look like red pushpins. If you take a seat, you'll be instantly turned into your five-year-old self as you twirl, wobble, and wiggle in a chair that won't sit still.

In my search for Ghoulardi T-shirts and Dirtbag Kipnis bobble-head dolls, **Room Service** (2078 W. 25th St.) was not exactly what I was looking for on my return trip to Cleveland, but it might perfectly fit your visit. The shop sells items you'll never find in Walmart, like organic baby bibs, Babe Body Soufflé Verbena Gypsy (rich hydrating and nourishing natural body cream), and an Eco Seed Starter (freshly muddled mint and lemon balm mojito with a cinnamon basil garnish). That all feels about as Cleveland to me as Russian nesting dolls or kimonos.

The elegant arcade at the Hyatt

The **Cuyahoga Collective** (15701 Madison Ave.) sells both produced and discovered goods from Ohio's North Shore. Sounding like an episode of *Man Shops Globe*, the TV show hosted by Anthropologie's Keith Johnson, they claim they are "a purveyor of goods and objects for the home. Our aesthetic represents the roamers and the seekers by taking inspiration from the North Coast and bridging the gap between home and exploration."

For me, their style and sensibility is a bit more Hamptons or Rodeo Drive than The Land, but I was tempted by their *PERCH Fish Fry* T-shirts.

STUFF TO BLOW UP

Well . . . it used to be "stuff to blow up" back in Ghoulardi days, when he stuffed lit M-80s inside plastic model kits and rubber frogs. Now, we just call them toys. There are several toy stores in The Land, two worth noting because they're not all Toys "R" Us mass produced or worse, "educational" toys.

★ ★ ★

Once Upon a Time (19285 Detroit Rd.) was originally located in downtown Cleveland's Old Arcade. They moved to Rocky River in 1988. Owner Jack Seelie founded the store to offer hand-picked domestic and imported toys made with quality and built to last as hand-me-downs. They sell imported Steiff teddy bears, but we will forgive them for also having some eco-friendly "Green Toys."

BIG FUN

Big Fun (1814 Coventry Rd.) has all the old Star Wars figures, Beavis and Butt-Head tattoos, and Ten Commandments sticky notes your inner jackanapes craves. Steve Presser opened Big Fun on April Fools' Day 1991. Over the years, he has bought his ever-refreshed stock from collectors and catalogs. The store, jammed with collectible toys, trading cards, magnets, T-shirts, trinkets, jokes, and gag gifts, looks like your childhood room where your mother would make you "clean up this mess!" before you could go outside to play.

More than toys, Big Fun has a vintage and treasured black and white photo booth. I collect old vertical photo booth strips, but they must be black and white and never with cute frames or backgrounds. Presser also sponsors events with local stars like Cleveland's Dr. U. R. Awesome, the Guinness World Record holder in two categories, largest indoor bubble and largest outdoor bubble. His best bubble was 834 cubic feet.

Most of all, the reason to go to Big Fun is owner Steve Presser. I would call him a Cleveland Essential.

Presser grew up in University Heights, and graduated from Cleveland Heights High School. He then studied pre-med at the University of Michigan. After graduating from college, Presser decided not to pursue a medical career. Instead, he started working for the Parents Volunteer Association, a nonprofit organization that provides care to people with disabilities. He left PVA in 1983 and took a job as a stockbroker at Paine Webber in Beachwood. This is hardly a career trajectory that leads to toy store owner.

He'd always been a lover and collector. His had been a childhood filled with '60s fandom and toys, *Lost in Space*, *The Man from U.N.C.L.E.*, *The Munsters*, and, his favorite, Rock 'em Sock 'em Robots. Steve's eyes light up when he recalls, "The one toy that I really wanted was a Johnny Seven Rocket OMA Rifle. OMA is for 'One Man Army.' This bad baby had all the bells and whistles that a little kid could ever want. It had a tommy gun, grenade launcher, automatic pistol, repeating rifle, anti-tank rocket, and armor-piercing shell/anti-bunker missile They ran a great TV commercial on it too, which fueled my wanting it. I have a December 30th birthday, so it was a Hanukkah/Christmas/birthday gift. I was in heaven when I got my Johnny Seven!"

The seeds to be a toy store owner were first sown, or in his case maybe we should say the pez pellets were first loaded, when Presser was on a trip to Chicago. He discovered a store called Goodies, later renamed Uncle Fun, and even later out of business. He says of the experience, "When I walked into the original Goodies, an amazingly jam-packed three-hundred-square-foot store, I lost it. Literally! Everything fired in my body and I had to sit down right on the floor. A kind staff person at the store noticed my situation and asked if everything was all right. I responded, 'Oh yes . . . Everything is REALLY all right!' That staff person was Ted Frankel, store owner and my eventual mentor in creating Big Fun. That summer day in 1982 was nothing short of a life-changing epiphany."

Into or nearing his sixties, Steve's boyish face also lights up when talking about Cleveland. "When I'm asked what I like most about Cleveland, I immediately respond . . . Clevelanders. Clevelanders, transplants, expats, and out-of-towners appreciate the good ol' days and what makes Cleveland special: ethnicity and authenticity."

As with any good Clevelander of a certain age, Ghoulardi was a huge influence. At age five or six, Steve got to hang out with the older kids and watch the horror host on Friday nights and later use his super power, blowing things up.

"Most of the kids on my street built models. They would spend literally hours assembling, gluing, and then painting them. After all their work and undoubtedly inspired by Ghoulardi, they loved having "Little Stevie" (a.k.a. me) blow up their Weird-Oh kits and their Aurora monster models. I was no good at model making, but I was great, a real six-year-old pyro pro, at blowing them up!"

CHAPTER TEN

Dyngus Days & Duct Tape Festivals

HOW CLEVELAND CELEBRATES

I've always been dead set against festivals—really suspicious and wary.

—Elton John

S A CLEVELANDER, IN WINTER MONTHS YOU WAKE UP MOST every day to gray; seemingly endless gray skies and snow hummocks turned to gray-colored slush. In such a Land parades and festivals the rest of the year are always a good idea.

While writing this book, I interviewed a Clevelander dedicated to marketing the city to vacation travelers, business travelers, meeting planners, and group travel planners. I felt the desire to continually edit her responses to my questions. Where she said, "I get irritated with vague and seemingly contradictory lists like *Forbes* magazine, which ranked us as one of the country's most miserable cities," I wanted to correct her, "Forbes didn't rank Cleveland as one of the most miserable cities, it ranked it as THE most miserable city."

Later, she said one of the biggest misconceptions about Cleveland was that it had terrible weather. Here, I felt, "Sorry, as one who lived in Cleveland twenty-two years, I can't let that statement go unchallenged. That response seems like textbook Stockholm Syndrome. Cleveland only doesn't have terrible weather when compared to the Gulag Archipelago or Vostok Station, Antarctica.

Growing up in Cleveland, I don't remember that many parades. I cut school with my neighbor Bennie Iacobucci, led astray by his dad, Big Ben Iacobucchi, for a St. Patrick's parade. Kids TV host Barnaby served as grand marshall. Barnaby wore a bright kelly green jacket that day, his habitual straw hat, and pointy ears, and I recall his face being unnaturally bright pink. Later we learned Barnaby had "issues," so maybe his pink face had less to do with the cold weather. I also remember Fourth of July concerts on the town square of Chagrin Falls where a band of middle-aged men would play songs like "Seventy-Six Trombones," "Stars & Stripes Forever," and "Anchors Aweigh." With the band's severe lack of talent, all the songs sounded pretty much the same.

And that was about it.

While writing this book, I have learned that Cleveland now rivals almost any city in celebrations.

Listed below are many of the annual festivals and parades in Cleveland around which you may want to plan and build your visit.

JANUARY

Not too many festivals in January, as The Land remains cold and gray.

North Coast Harbor Ice Fest displays outdoor ice sculptures and provides ice sculpting lessons should you ever want a side career making decorations for lowbrow galas.

At the **Cleveland Beer Fest** you can sample more than four hundred fresh craft beers of all styles. Collected funds are given to the Music Education Society, a nonprofit dedicated to helping music programs in underfunded elementary and junior high schools. Seems as good a reason as any to get drunk.

FEBRUARY

There is still not too much in the way of festivals. Still too cold and gray.

But, acting like Polar Bear Plunge members, Clevelanders strip down to their undies for a race beginning at the House of Blues and winding through East 9th Street and Prospect Avenue. The **Cupid Undie Run** is held in seventy cities each February. In Orlando, Los Angeles, and Phoenix, that's not a big deal. In Cleveland, Detroit, and Buffalo, that shows real commitment. Cleveland draws about seven hundred undie runners each year. Proceeds go to the Children's Tumor Foundation.

House of Blues also sponsors several local music and beer events. There's a **House of Blues Local Brew Party** in San Diego, Houston, Orlando, Dallas, and Cleveland. For the $35 pass you get twenty samplings of beer or food. It's not held every year, so check their calendar.

The Donut Fest is held in three other cities in addition to Cleveland—NYC, Chicago, and Dallas. Bakeries in each city submit their best glazed or jelly-filled to compete for the coveted title of "Best Donut." Clevelanders pretty universally feel the best donut shop is Jack Frost Donuts (4960 Pearl Rd.). Opened in 1937, they bake from scratch every day, using age-old methods.

Brite Winter Festival, held in Ohio City, features a bonfire with marshmallows, a wintry mini-golf course, plus food, beverages, and live music, all in the bitter outdoors.

Each year, the first actually cool festival that's Cleveland-centric and not for Anytown, USA, is **Kurentovanje** (pronounced koo-rahn-toh-VAHN-yay for non-Slovenian readers). The Kurent is a character from Slovenian lore who chases away the winter and ushers in the spring. BTW, there are more Slovenians in Cleveland than anywhere in the world except for Ljubljana, the capital of Slovenia. Kurent looks like some mad scientist has spliced together the genes of an alpaca, a mountain goat, a shag rug, and a little Donald Trump (the Kurent always wears an ugly red tie).

Cleveland's Kurentovanje is filled with costumes, a parade, ethnic food, drink, and music—and what's a winter festival without ice carving? There's always the Kurent Jump, where costumed characters start their task of scaring snow and ice into puddled submission.

MARCH

Still not too many fests, as Cleveland's winters tend not to be intimidated by people jumping around dressed as shag rugs with Trump ties.

I've been to the **Lago Festival** site, and I still have no idea what it is. Their online copy states, "Winter weather and seasonal depression have had their fun, so let's celebrate as if it's really summer in Cleveland, Ohio," and, "Live music performances that are best enjoyed in as little clothing as possible (but please wear clothes)." So, that sounds like . . . umm . . . maybe fun?

APRIL

As winter hangs on for yet another month, festivals are not your #1 reason to come to Cleveland in April. The city averages 2.5 inches of snow each April.

The one, the only April festival I could find is the **Haiku Death Match**. Each year pits the region's best writers of the Japanese seventeen-syllable form against each other. Poets read their original Haiku in a much less confrontational rap battle. The last poet standing is declared Haiku Death Match Master.

While not a festival, you can venture to Lyndhurst, an Eastside suburb, to see **Eggshelland**. Eggshelland features thousands of colorful, hand-painted eggshells arranged into religious montages and cartoon characters. For fifty-six years, Ron and Betty Manolio used forty-thousand hand-painted shells each year to create displays on their lawn every Easter season. When Ron died in 2012, Betty said it was the last Eggshelland.

Then, the Euclid Beach Boys promised to preserve the tradition. The Boys are a group dedicated to "Preserving Cleveland's Amusement History, One Piece at a Time." They have an **Event Center & Museum** (156 Euclid Square Mall Dr.) open Tuesdays through Thursdays 1 p.m. to 7 p.m.

You'll have to dig a bit to see where Eggshelland is each year. One year Eggshelland was displayed at the Lyndhurst tennis courts. Another year, the exhibit was presented between a Crate & Barrel store and Tropical Smoothie Cafe.

Almost a companion piece, Steve Kaselak's **Jellybeanville** has been on display forty-six years. He decorates his home on Zeman Avenue in Euclid each Easter season, inspired by Al Yockey. Al had been the neighborhood "egg man," delivering eggs to local homes. Yockey used to install an annual Easter egg display.

When Kaselak took on the tradition years later, he wanted each year's display to be bigger than the year before. He hustles to have his elaborate Jellybeanville completed by Palm Sunday. Requiring a much needed day of rest, Kaselak takes Easter Sunday off and is nowhere to be seen. On that day, there is the Easter Bunny himself, standing in Kaselak's yard, handing out baskets of goodies to the kids and ready to pose for photo ops for visitors.

The day after Easter is known as **Dyngus Day**. The Polish tradition celebrates the end of Lent. It traces its origins back to the baptism of Polish Prince Mieszko in 966 A.D. with water hurled about to signify cleaning and purification. A traditional event has single boys chasing single girls to douse them with water. Current Dyngus Days use squirt guns in place of buckets. The girls get their chance a week later when they get to hurl plates at the boys. It all seems vaguely symbolic of the stages of courtship and marriage.

While celebrated in many Polish American communities, Cleveland's version of Dyngus is reportedly "the best," with polka jam sessions and an accordion parade.

MAY

May, which some years is the first month without snow, is chock full of festivals. Clevelanders, delighted to put away their snow shovels, rock salt, and tire chains, are ready to celebrate Asian culture, Greeks, Irish, Reggae music, BBQ ribs, and being a hippie.

The **Hessler Street Fair** has been called "Cleveland's timeless hippie festival," which makes me wonder, which is it? You can't be both "timeless" and a movement thoroughly locked into the mid-'60s. The Hessler Neighborhood Association was formed in 1969 to save the neighborhood from being razed to create dormitories for Case Western University. Hessler Road is listed in the National Register of Historic Places. The adjoining Hessler Court is the only remaining street in Cleveland and one of only five in America that is still made with Nicolson pavement. Nicolson pavement is wood block and was briefly popular in the 1820s. It fell into disfavor because it's hard to maintain and treacherously slippery in wet or icy weather. Cleveland's weather is nothing if not wet or icy.

An estimated ten thousand attend each year's outdoor festival. All proceeds are used to preserve and maintain the neighborhood. The two-day event has continuous music from 11 a.m. until well after dark, with locally known groups like Cats On Holiday.

The timeless hippie fest also includes arts and crafts vendors, vegetarian food, and street performances like Faith McFluff, who combines fire eating with hula hoop artistry.

The **Asian Festival** takes place at Asia Plaza and East 27th

Street. The Festival was created in 2008 by Johnny Wu to show off this lesser-known neighborhood, which has five Asian groceries. The festival reportedly draws fifty thousand people (that feels like a misprint or massive exaggeration) and celebrates the food, music, and culture of the Chinese, Taiwanese, Korean, Japanese, Filipino, Indian, Vietnamese, Cambodian, Laotian, Thai, Karen, Hmong, and Bhutanese. I hear the Mea Datshi (Bhutan's national dish) is delicious.

The **Tremont Greek Festival** nears fifty-five years. The four-day festival is held at the St. Constantine and Helen Greek Orthodox Cathedral (3352 Mayfield Road) and celebrates everything Greek, with music performed by what the fest calls "Authentic Greek Bands" (as opposed to those lame Greek Tribute Bands), Hellenic dancers in traditional garb, and Greek food like pastitsio, moussaka, spanakopita, and tiropita. There are two pastry booths selling baklava and galatobouriko. Free cooking classes are offered if you want to learn how to prepare any of these dishes you cannot pronounce.

"Hooley" is an Irish word for party. **Hooley on Kamm's Corners** is an annual festival with a full day of traditional Irish entertainment such as karate and pony rides, accented by famed Irish food like gyros, hot dogs, pulled pork, and kettle corn. Well, at least the music tends toward Irish, with the Pipes and Drums of the Cleveland Police, Cleveland Firefighters Memorial Pipes and Drums, and the not-to-be-missed Pogues tribute band, The Boys From the County Hell.

The Boys were formed one night when members were sitting in a car in a Taco Bell line. When the Pogues came on the radio, Doug "Texas Terry" McKean thought it'd be cool to form a tribute band if only to play every St. Patrick's Day. They now approach their thirtieth year as a band, i.e., exceeding the life span of the actual Pogues.

Twinsburg, Ohio, a suburb of Cleveland, is best known for

its Twins Day, held each August. The **Reggae Festival** can be seen as sort of Twinsburg's warm-up act. The music fest is held at the Perici Amphitheatre, called a hidden gem. Accompanying the music will be Barrio Tacos food truck and Betty's Bad Ass Burgers.

The **Found Footage Festival** made its way from Eau Claire, WI, through Minneapolis, Pittsburgh, Los Angeles, and Tucson, with a stop in Cleveland. Each year celebrates weird and funky old film clips of things like Arnold Schwarzenegger going wild at Carnival in Rio, instructional videos of how to have better sex through hypnosis, and outtakes from thirty years of the David Letterman show. It's like a communal viewing of the Best of YouTube.

At the end of May, Chagrin Falls holds the **Blossom Time Festival** right off Main Street next to the Chagrin River. It's an old-fashioned town festival with undersized rides, games of chance, corn dogs, and cotton candy. The festival is a harmless Midwestern event where a sixteen-year-old boy might sneak a kiss behind the Fun House after he knocks over some wooden milk bottles and wins a girl a giant purple bear.

JUNE

The highlight of June, or really most any month in Cleveland, is the **Avon Heritage Duck Tape Festival**. It is a three-day event in the self-proclaimed duct tape capital of the world—Avon, Ohio—and the home of Duck brand duct tape. There are Rose Bowl–like parades, where rather than flowers and seeds, the floats are made entirely of—you guessed it—duct tape. There are duct tape fashion shows, where I assume runway models have a much harder time slipping in and out of various dresses. There are arts and crafts booths where you can make your own duct tape jewelry or wall hangings where no nails are needed. About the only thing you won't see are duct tape tacos or deep fried duct tape on a stick. Though, I may have just prompted some vendors for next year's festival.

Larchmere PorchFest is a free music festival featuring local bands performing on the front porches of homes on and near Larchmere Boulevard on Cleveland's east side. Thirty porches—thirty bands.

The **Cleveland Pizza Festival**, at the Cuyahoga County Fairgrounds, is a more standard food festival like you'd find in Anytown, USA. Mariano "Mushmouth" Pachetti was the Jim Brown of pizza eating. He could devour an entire pie in under two minutes. No one could beat Pachetti until he was dethroned by the Fairview Fireball in 1972. Fireball was a (probably starved for days) German shepherd.

The **Tater Tots & Beer Festival**, like the Winter Jam, Found Footage, and Donut Festival, is not just a Cleveland thing. There are tater tot fests more than seventy cities. Each fest is three hours of drinking beer and stuffing tots. It started in 2015 as someone's idea of the perfect food and alcohol pairing. Me? I'd advocate for a Grilled Tuna and Swiss Sandwich and Hard Lemonade Fest, but I doubt many people would attend.

The **Random Hero Festival** (my favorite name for a festival) is a tribute to the late Ryan Dunn, an actor/comedian best known for his work with the *Jackass* crowd in movies and the TV series. Held at the Agora Theater, the event features headbanging bands like Mushroomhead, Official CKY, and Bam Margera's Fuckface Unstoppable. Again, I don't know Bam Margera's Fuckface Unstoppable, but I admire the name of the band and the titles of their songs like "Bend My Dick" and "Shitbird Serenade."

Then, there's **Parade the Circle**, which is for many THE favorite Cleveland festival. For twenty-five years, Parade the Circle has transformed University Circle into an artsy free-for-all parade of movable art, giant puppets, and dressed-to-the-nines stilt walkers. Artists go wild with papier-mâché, clay, fabric, and wood, all painted and glued to become giant flowers and monkey puppets, all Julie Taymor–quality characters. Past parades have included walking martinis and one hundred Marilyn Monroe tribute artists.

The parade began as a community outreach experiment by the art museum to festively mark its seventy-fifth anniversary. It has grown from a few hundred observers to now more than seventy-five thousand parade watchers, making it one of Cleveland's biggest and most stunning annual events.

JULY

The **Cain Park Arts Festival** takes place, of all places, in Cain Park (14591 Superior Rd.). It has been called "an arts-sensory overload" with more than 150 artists performing folk, bluegrass, and jazz, plus fast-food vendors and craft makers.

The first **Big Little Comedy Festival** in 2010 had seventeen acts and was held in Grand Rapids, MI. By 2013, it had grown too large for Grand Rapids and moved to Cleveland. It's now a full week of the region's top improv groups, sketch comedy troupes, stand-up comics, and online filmmakers. There are also workshops conducted by some of the top comedy instructors.

For most Clevelanders, Little Italy is the renowned Italian neighborhood. Since forming in 1925, Mount Carmel is the West Side's equivalent. Each July, the neighborhood's church holds the **Our Lady of Mount Carmel Italian Festival**. It's five days of free events, offering nightly live entertainment, rides acceptable to six-year-olds, Italian cuisine, and various games, including daily hold'em tournaments, which I'll assume are more Turin than Texas.

Not to be outdone, the **La Sagrada Familia Latin American Festival** celebrates Latin American traditions and heritage. The festival features nightly live entertainment, rides acceptable to six-year-olds, authentic Latin cuisine, and various games. I know nothing about Guatemala hold'em.

Not to be outdone, the **Irish Heritage Cuyahoga County Fair** is a three-day celebration with Irish bands, Irish dancers, Irish boxers, Irish art, Irish history, and, the show stopper, the Dogs Native to Ireland Parade, starring Irish wolfhounds, Irish water spaniels, Irish terriers, and frenetic Irish setters jostling at the rear.

Great Lakes Medieval Faire is seven miles south on I-90 in Rock Creek. It's family fun from the thirteenth century. You can watch demonstrations of hand-blown glass art, jewelers threading fine gold wire around exquisite crystals and jewels, clothiers, soap makers, and sword makers, all of which can be purchased and thereafter collect dust in your attic or garage. You can witness brave knights, off work for the weekend from their jobs at Best Buy or AutoZone, battle for the fair damsel wearing New Balances or Crocs under her gown.

Mid-July is the **Taste of Tremont**. The neighborhood holds a fair on Professor Street that showcases the best of Tremont's food, art, and entertainment. This is the hub of culinary genius, sprouting the likes of Michael Symon, Zach Bruell, Dante Bocuzzi, and Eric Williams.

The **Burning River Fest** is sponsored by Great Lakes Brewery and the Burning River Foundation (the latter was created to provide grants and resources for the sustainable future of Cleveland's waterways). In keeping with the spirit of the event, only those food vendors who have a commitment to organic sourcing and sustainability can participate. This does include the Pierogi Lady, who attends each year.

Food is secondary to beer during the Burning River Fest. Great Lakes Brewing Co. will pour their award-winning brews practically nonstop all weekend long. Great Lakes Brewing was founded in 1986 by brothers, Patrick and Daniel Conway, in a city and a state which at the time had no brewpubs and microbreweries. After selling less than one thousand barrels their first year, they passed the one-hundred-thousand-barrel mark in 2010.

AUGUST

Early August seems to draw out most every ethnicity in Cleveland not covered in July.

The annual Little Italy **Feast of the Assumption** has been at it nearing 120 years. It's a lively, four-day mix of religious observance, food fest, street carnival, and arts fair.

The oldest Romanian parish in America, founded in 1904, rolls out a virtual excursion to the Old Country. The three-day party comes with folk dancers, bands, and church tours. You can sink your fangs into a piece of mamaliga (a cheesy cornbread delicacy) and mineral water direct from Transylvania.

Pokrova Ukrainian Festival, **St. Mary Romanian Festival**, and the **Latino Arts and Culture Celebration of Greater Cleveland and Annual Puerto Rican Parade** round out the ethnic entertainment.

Garlic knows no national boundaries. Cleveland's **Garlic Festival** features much more than garlic. There's the far from traditional garlic tractor pull. You can check out Flower the Clown, whom I've never experienced but to me looks online to be about as amusing as paper cuts, or Outback Ray, Cleveland's latest safari clad animal handler. It was Jungle Larry in my childhood who would appear on kiddie TV shows or events with his massive pythons and adorable hedgehogs.

To eat you can get everything from your garlic fries to Mitchell's Garlic Ice Cream. Each festival will crown a Top Chef and the annual Miss Garlic. My guess is being chosen Miss Garlic does not immediately get the girl a slew of additional dates.

Warehouse District Street Festival causes West Sixth

Street to be shut down by a traffic jam of food vendors, arts and crafts booths, and live bands the first weekend in August. The festival represents cuisines of Japan, Lebanon, Italy, Portugal, Brazil, Mexico, Greece, and America. For entertainment, there'll be putt-putt, performing robots, magicians, jugglers, and acrobat performers known as the Jasmine Dragons. To be all things to all people, the fest also includes a cutest dog contest and fashion show.

St. Casimir was a church the Cleveland Diocese closed in 2009. Encouraged by a dream of one of the parishioners, other members of the congregation would come daily to the locked gates and pray. Eventually the Vatican finally gave in and allowed the church to reopen. **Taste of St. Casimir's Polish Festival** is a weekend-long festival where you can eat pierogi, kielbasa, stuffed cabbage, or the lesser known chleb ze smalcem (lard spread on bread).

Since 1976, Twinsburg has had the world's largest gathering of twins for **Twins Day**. Twinsburg was founded by identical twins Aaron and Moses Wilcox. In addition to being born on the same day, they died on the same day, October 25, 1827.

The festival is a one day twinanza of look-alike contests, the Double Take Parade, entertainment (including the Twin Talent Show), and a lot of people wearing matching T-shirts.

The **Cuyahoga County Fair** has been around since 1893. I imagine back then it was farmers dressed in overalls and straw hats trying to get a good price on herefords and holsteins, years later replaced by farmers in John Deere caps and boot-cut jeans doing pretty much the same thing. Somewhere along the way, the County Fair started attracting as many ironic urban hipsters, and it now features pig races, tractor pulls, and demolition derbies. You can also test your skill and resolve in a stare-down contest with a rooster. When you lose, you can rationalize to yourself, "Yeah, but that rooster gets to practice every day!" Everyone else will still be thinking, "Yeah, but you lost to a chicken."

Weapons of Mass Creation is a festival for creativity in Cleveland, founded in 2010. It's kind of a Cleveland take on the TED Conference or SXSW. Speakers talk about design, creativity, entrepreneurship, community, activism, and pursuing happiness in creative endeavors.

The **Carnival of Madness** is an annual hard rock/alternative rock tour, also founded in 2010. The festival has a carnival theme, with artists and bands sharing the event with circus performers and fire breathers.

SEPTEMBER

The **Festival of Saint Rocco** has been held for more than one hundred years, always at the church in Cleveland's oldest Italian parish. The Fest is known for Monday's famous greased pole climb. Spectators crowd round to see who, if anyone, can make it to the top of an old wooden utility pole, heavily slathered with axle grease. The Fest is more loved for the homemade meatballs, lasagne, and zeppoli.

St. John Cantius Polish Festival is a celebration of Polish heritage. Guests can enjoy polka performances, sample authentic traditional Polish dishes, and play a variety of outdoor games. The current church, designed by architects Gabele & Potter, in what is often called the Polish Cathedral Style, was erected on the same site in 1925.

IngenuityFest is Cleveland's annual celebration of art, performances, and technology. Held in Docks 32 and 30, located north of the Cleveland Browns' stadium, the two warehouses have more than 120,000 square feet of indoor space along with ample outdoor space and stunning views of the city.

The Cleveland Museum of Art sponsors the annual **Chalk Festival**, now running some twenty-plus years. Following a sixteenth-century Italian tradition, the festival allows attendees to create their section of sidewalk as part of a streetscape of chalk masterpieces.

OCTOBER

The **HUMP Film Festival** is a national event which also plays in thirty-two other cities. The festival features short dirty movies—each less than five minutes—all created by people who aren't porn stars but want to be one for a weekend. Sounds absolutely terrifying.

GhoulardiFest is an annual fan event going into its twelfth year. It was most recently held at the the LaVilla Party and Conference Center, described as "conveniently located near I-77 and I-71and just off of I-480, minutes from the airport," and it has costume contests, pizza fights, and what they call Scaryaoke. The website calls it a "whacky weekend festival," which already broadcasts it to be exactly the type of totally uncool event Ernie Anderson would never attend and of which he might have said, "Hey Group. This fest is so bad, you should just keep driving down I-480."

The annual **Woollybear Festival** is held in downtown Vermilion, Ohio, about forty-five minutes from Cleveland. It is touted as Ohio's largest one-day festival . . . held between the hours of 10 a.m. and 7 p.m. . . . devoted to a caterpillar.

The event began in 1973, the brainchild of Dick Goddard, a Cleveland TV weatherman. Goddard is like Cleveland's version of Al Roker or Willard Scott, except less the New York gascon and more of a Mr. Rogers type. Much the same way Punxsutawney Phil is celebrated on Groundhog Day, the woolly bear caterpillar is similarly celebrated for its mythical association with winter forecasting. After the caterpillars' eggs hatch in the Fall, folklore suggests the severity of an upcoming winter can be gauged by the amount of black versus orange in the caterpillars' bands.

The fest now draws more than twenty marching bands, two thousand marchers, hundreds of animals, and tens upon tens of thousands of spectators. There is a woolly bear costume contest for both people and their pets, all dressed up as woolly bear caterpillars. The Sunday festival changes dates each year to line up with the Browns having an away game.

And then, of course, there's **Halloween**. Some years an early cold snap practically ruins Halloween for unhappy kids, forced to wear lumpy winter coats over their zombie, vampire, and Batman costumes.

Cleveland does not quite match the annual destruction that Detroit exercises each Halloween, when Motown residents do their best to burn down the city on what they call Devil Night. Cleveland's mischief dates back to 1897, when a group of ax-wielding boys chopped down a twenty-three-foot-high fence. D.Z. Herr had constructed the eyesore in a dispute with his neighbor, Mr. Moon. Moon had raised a barn, causing Herr to erect the absurdly high wall to block the view.

My Halloweens growing up were mostly about going door to door, hoping for Baby Ruths and Reese's Peanut Butter Cups and more often getting the much dreaded apples or pennies. There was a local tradition in which (I swear) I never participated where destructive kids would roll pumpkins and the occasional bowling ball down the very steep hill of Main Street into the downtown shopping district of Chagrin Falls. Broken storefront windows and car windshields welcomed residents the next morning.

NOVEMBER

Getting a jump on the really miserable weather, **Cleveland Winterfest** is held on Public Square in November. It features a holiday pop-up shop of indie crafts, food trucks, and a Winterfest Children's Stage featuring music, interactive activities, and performances from kid-friendly theatrical group the Talespinner Children's Theatre. The full day of activities concludes at 6 p.m. with an hour-long holiday lighting ceremony, which features a visit from Santa, fireworks display, and music from Spazmatics, an especially awful and intentionally nerdy '80s dance band.

Genghis Con, an award-winning small press and underground comic convention, is always held on the Sunday after Thanksgiving. There are hundreds if not thousands of other comic conventions, including SuperCon, MegaCon, Super Megafest Con, FantastiCon, TerrifiCon, and the most super and mega, the International Comic-Con held in San Diego, which draws roughly 150,000 attendees each year.

Most cons focus on fandom and mainstream pop culture. Genghis Con, as claimed on their website, "has been, and will always be, about the D.I.Y. ethic and the Independent, Underground Culture that maintains to be a place that fosters fresh, new ideas and the opportunity for more personal, open engagement between the creators and their readers."

DECEMBER

Cleveland is one of eleven cities participating in the **Ugly Sweater Run**. The 5K run is presented by Kahlúa. Finishers receive an Ugly Sweater Run knit hat, and they claim "an after party like no other!" Contests including Best Ugly Sweater, Best Pet Attire, Team Outfits, Most Inappropriate Sweater, Largest Group/Family in similar sweaters, Best Beard, and Best Fake Beard.

Mr. Kringle's Inventionasium Experience is an experience that is profoundly a Cleveland-only thing. Between mid-November and Christmas Eve, families enter the Tower City Center (230 W. Huron Rd.), at first greeted by Eyesly, a dapper gentleman in suit and top hat with just a giant eyeball for a head. You'll be given lab coats before being led through a maze of bright neon rooms with *Twin Peaks*–style checkered floors by a series of guides with names like Rhubarb Hiccup and Charolette Hollyhop. Each stop is set up to create imaginative (weird) toys. In the Brainstorming Room, you're given magic foam to create squishy toys. In other rooms, you'll make toys and puppets of out thing-amajigs and whatsits. Along the way there are instant messages (in the form of scrolls) and magic tricks. There's a snow-making laboratory where you will grow your own snow, because the fifty-seven inches Cleveland gets each winter just aren't enough. And finally, you'll meet The Fat Man himself.

Jimmy Langa created the Inventionasium Experience in 2007 to make Christmas more interesting to modern (jaded) kids. It's certainly a departure from my old Mr. Jingeling. The whole experience feels like the love child that would result if Dr. Seuss and Pee Wee Herman were in a ménage à trois with Tim Burton.

Conclusion

Who we are cannot be separated from where we're from.

—Malcolm Gladwell

*A*FTER A LIFETIME OF RUNNING FROM THOSE WHITE PICKET fences and food (formerly) without flavor, I have finally embraced my Clevelandness.

Plato wrote, "What is honored in a culture will be cultivated there." New York City honors aggressiveness and being one step ahead of the competition. New York City is a bastion of skyscrapers, massive egos, and a neurotic energy (which can be quite intoxicating) to keep up with the hot new restaurant, hot new play, and hot new neighborhood to live. Charleston and Savannah honor bloodlines and tradition. If your family roots don't go back at least three generations, you're not *really* from Charleston or Savannah.

As much as I honor Tennessee Williams, he simply got it wrong when he famously said, "America has only three cities: New York, San Francisco, and New Orleans. Everywhere else is Cleveland."

Cleveland's is an absolutely unique culture that embraces its shortcomings and relishes in its goofiness. Sure, Clevelanders have grown tired of the burning river jokes. It has been fifty years. Eddie Murphy and Jim Carey lost their comedic edge in much less time. But there is a part of most Clevelanders that takes a perverse pride that they're from the city where the river caught on fire. Who wouldn't prefer that over the cute touristy San Antonio Riverwalk or Savannah's River Street?

Cleveland takes a delight in the disaster of 10 cent beer night. As painful as The Drive and The Fumble and Red Right 88, there is a sweetness to the suffering that is part of the city's character. Jacksonville, Houston, and San Diego teams lose consistently, but in boring, "We'll get 'em next time" ways. Cleveland has lost in some of the most heart-wrenching, never-get-over-it ways that border on high tragedy.

Other cities' fans simply stop coming to games. Eagles fans grow nasty and pick fights with everyone, including the halftime Santa Claus. In Cleveland, it's not about gritting your teeth and trying harder. It's not about finding something else to do on a Sunday. Here Browns fans wear shirts stating "Rebuilding Since 1964" as they fill "The Factory of Sadness."

In most other cities, Mayor Ralph Perk would have been laughed out of town after setting his hair on fire at a ribbon-cutting ceremony, or weighing whether to have dinner with the President of the United States or show up for the weekly bowling night. Here, he served a second and then a third term.

There's an ironic embrace of our shortcomings, but it's laced with the hint of hope. Maybe someday Cleveland will return to the vibrancy of Millionaires' Row, or the days when it was the oil refinery capital or the automobile capital—we would settle for being the mob car bombing capital once again. Maybe someday the Browns will win back-to-back games.

All of those marketing firms that came up with "Cleveland's the Plum" or "Cleveland Rocks!" miss the point. Cleveland is not Hotlanta or the Raleigh-Durham Research Triangle, wanting to be seen as the shiny new thing. Cleveland is not hip like Austin, Texas, or Portland, Oregon, and it doesn't seek to be. Cleveland doesn't cover up its warts or craggy teeth. Cleveland embraces its Rust Belt flawed and fragmentary parts.

Cleveland will always be the place where I had my first "real" kiss. I got so flustered kissing Joni Trinetti in her driveway, I took my foot off the brake and nearly drove into her backyard. Cleveland will be the place where my mother forced me to go on my first-ever date, taking a friend-of-the-family girl to the Blossom

The chandelier in Cleveland's theatre district

Festival. The night took a turn when we were riding the Tilt-A-Whirl and Bill Nesbit suddenly threw up. Most of us were able to avoid what looked like Campbell's Chunky Soup in outer space. But not the girl I was forced to bring. The side of her face and her hair were covered in whatever Bill Nesbit had for dinner. She ran home and I got to enjoy the Blossom Festival unencumbered. Cleveland is the place where I went to Saturday monster movie matinees at the Mapletown Theater and one time ran screaming into the lobby when my brother told me King Kong reaches out into the audience and eats a few kids. Cleveland is where I discovered Santa wasn't real when I found "his" special wrapping paper (tissue paper with flecks of gold) hidden at the top of my sister's closet. I would years later use the same hiding space to store torn-out photographs of Cynthia Myers, Claudia Jennings, and other Playmates of the '60s. Cleveland is where every Thursday night during high school football season I would close myself up in my bedroom, put on headphones, and crank up the volume to *Hall of the Mountain King* and the soundtrack for *In Harm's Way* to get myself ready to wage holy war on whatever team we played the next night. Cleveland is where I once stayed up most of the night trying to be the X caller into a radio station to get free tickets to a Monkees concert. Cleveland is where I sat in the shallow end of my backyard pool one night with friends and we all saw what was unquestionably a UFO. After it darted around and eventually flew by us at unbelievable speed, Chuck Ohlrich said, "We never saw that and I never want to talk about it." Cleveland is where I watched Browns games in the old stadium with terrible sight lines, painfully uncomfortable wooden slat seats, but which was always beautifully packed to the rafters with middle-aged men, smelling of cigars and wearing gray or black overcoats, fedora hats, and no team logos anywhere. Their stirring cheer of "Go! Go! Go!" will forever be so much better than the piped in clutter of "Who Let the Dogs Out" or "We Are the Champions." Cleveland is where I found Phoebe, my six-month-old puppy, drowned under the pool cover. I still cannot allow myself to re-experience that moment in any direct way. Cleveland is where I thumb-wrestled Sue Reinthal in the eighth grade. I nearly passed out, holding her soft hand. I can still see the tiny ring on her finger, shaped like a daisy with gold leaves and a spot of yellow paint to represent the floret. Cleveland is where I'd sometimes be left alone when my parents went out to a party and I'd exchange clear lightbulbs for red ones and put Jimi Hendrix or Cream on my father's record playing console, which was the size of a couch, and blast at full bass and full volume. Cleveland is where I pursued a girl because she was hauntingly beautiful but then got so much more than I bargained when she turned out to be brilliant and "made" me read *A Perfect Day for Bananafish* and *Bartleby the Scrivener*. I hated reading before then, because horrible high school teachers drained all the joy out of books. Cleveland is the place where I woke up one night to a loud bang on Interstate 271, which ran two blocks from my bedroom window. We learned the next day it was a couple, married that day, struck late at night by a drunk driver racing down the wrong side of the highway with his lights off. Everyone was killed. There was something almost Shakespearean about the horribleness of the young couple's death. Their mangled cars sat in the lot of a gas station at Brainard Road and Chagrin Boulevard for days. Driving by, I'd sort of half peek out my car window, both hoping to see and hoping not to see bloodied evidence of the tragedy.

What I realize now in my sixties is that these random events nudged me or jostled me in new directions, but always through the filter of a core me, a core me created by growing up in the specific time and the exact place of Cleveland.

That spirit infects anyone who grew up there. My own sensibility I now recognize as pure Cleveland. Reviews of my previous books characterize my writing as "irreverent," "playful," or "intentionally over-the-top." Shaped by Cleveland, how could it be otherwise?

If I had to christen Cleveland with yet another new nickname, it might be City of Poetry. At the close of the movie *The Commitments*, the ragtag Irish band gives a practically perfect concert, and then backstage their usual bickering explodes and the band breaks up. Joey the Lips Fagan, sort of the soul and spokesperson for the band, tells the manager, "Yeah, we could have made albums and gone on to be famous. But that way would have been predictable. This way—it's poetry."

Cleveland could have beaten the Broncos or the Raiders and gone onto the Super Bowl. I like to believe that if they'd hung onto Belichick and Saban, they would have won several. The Indians could have won one of their Game 7 extra inning World Series games. If they sold to Steinbrenner rather than Mileti, they would have won several. If Alexander Winton had just hired Henry Ford, Cleveland would be the motor city. If the city had hung onto its aeronautic engineers, the famous NASA phrase would now be, "Cleveland, we have a problem." If we hadn't chased John D. Rockefeller away, maybe it'd be New York City calling itself the Big Plum.

There are so many near misses and not quites in Cleveland's history. But this way—it's poetry.

Acknowledgments

I NEED TO THANK MY HOSTS AND GUIDES WHO HELPED ME WHEN I returned to Cleveland: Erin O'Brien, a gifted writer whose passion for and quirky focus upon The Land is unsurpassed; Suzanne DeGaetano, a plugged-in and passionate bookseller; Steve Presser, a passionate purveyor of toys, memorabilia, and all things Cleveland; Bob Perkoski, a truly gifted photographer; Brian Meggett, of the Cleveland Public Library, who painstakingly set aside archival files for me to peruse during my visit; Louis McClung, a man with the unusual passion of restoring old religious statues; and several of my old high school buddies, including John Flower, a passionate juggler—sometimes while hurling down a mountainside on skis—Mike Gleason, my old fellow captain of the football team, who gave me his prime seats for "Dirtbag" Kipnis bobblehead night; fellow footballer with equally miserable knees, Doug Musgrave; Libby Post (Haffey), an old high school crush and her husband, Ken (I know Ken, and I drove Libby crazy driving around the city with our male DNA need to recall the heights and weights of all of the '64 Browns' starters); and my great friend since kindergarten, Rich Ward.

A special thank you to my daughter, Ella, and my son, Austin. Finally, I must thank my wife, Marnie Carmichael, my true soul-mate.

𝒥𝓃𝒹𝑒𝓍